The Ideal Quitter

Entrepreneurship lessons worth Half a million USD

Md. Mubir M. Chowdhury

Copyright © 2020 Md. Mubir M. Chowdhury

All rights reserved.

ISBN: 9781713348498

Version: 1.1 (updated: 12th April 2020)

DEDICATION

To all the budding entrepreneurs hassling to build a better tomorrow…

ACKNOWLEDGMENTS

I want to thank the almighty Allah for giving me the opportunity and capability to write this book. I would like to thank my parents and in-laws for their physical support throughout my entrepreneurial journey along with kind words, blessings, and prayers. I also thank my wife and son for sharing the challenges of being an early level entrepreneur's family member and sacrificing their comfort while I am busy in chasing my dreams.

PREFACE

Entrepreneurship! It is the new buzz word! We feel enticed by all the cool stories floating in social media about raising millions of dollars investment and the charming stories of young billionaires. Responding to this anticipation, a good lot of people are quitting jobs to start their businesses. They get inspired by notions like 'being my own boss', 'freedom of work', and 'build my empire.' Sadly, many of these neo-entrepreneurs are doing so without a holistic evaluation of the days ahead. In some cases, they are quitting their dreams shortly and getting back to jobs after facing hardships. In the process, a very crucial time of their career is lost and maybe even their lifelong savings!

I have been living the life of an entrepreneur since 2013 when I decided to quit my ten years-long corporate career. In the years to follow, I Co-founded two startups. The first one is an IT firm followed by another customer experience management consultancy firm (where I worked as the CEO). My IT firm created two award-winning software applications. It bagged us the identity as one of the top ten IT startups of Bangladesh by the government, along with winning international accolades like being Champion in the Seedstars World Bangladesh chapter, and winning BRAC Manthan Digital Innovation Award, mBillionth South Asia Award etc.

Amongst severe financial constraints and far from considering myself a 'success', these entrepreneurship years have been greatly rewarding. I got mental satisfaction, gained insights into seeing the world in a new light, and found new friends. This entrepreneurial journey has helped me to gain more self-confidence and learn how to survive outside the corporate cushion and apparent social security! I've seen uncertainties being handled in such a consistent manner that now I'm even a better follower of God! The joy you get from small successes as an entrepreneur cannot be compared to anything. The independence and freedom are not even grasped by a regular 9 to 5 job holder.

THE IDEAL QUITTER

First I wrote a small article on LinkedIn about a few of my learnings as a 'job quitting entrepreneur. It received a fairly good review from the readers. Some even asked me to write in-depth in the form of a book, exposing the hardships that are seldom talked about by most entrepreneurship enthusiasts and evangelists. This has greatly inspired me to start writing this book.

In this book, I have shed light on the lessons I have learned over the first five years of my entrepreneurial journey. Getting to know these well in advance should help a new or maybe even a not-so-new entrepreneur to foresee what might be next to come. To put down in words my journey narrated here, I had to spend more than USD 500,000 over this period excluding my opportunity cost. It took me around two years to complete writing this book in between firefighting my day to day huddle of managing a small business.

I truly hope that reading this book will help you as an existing or potential entrepreneur. I hope it will be a guide to jumpstart your business with as little mistakes as possible and get on the right track in the least possible time. I dream this book will be the first stepping stone for millions of people on their entrepreneurial journey and be an integral part of it.

I would like to put in my 'disclaimer' that all the lessons put in this book reflect my perspective and you may not agree with a few of those. The objective of my book is not to 'teach' you but to rather make you think of the 'possibilities' of the points discussed. As most of the points are generic, any type of entrepreneur can relate to it, be it a job holder or a fresh graduate.

I've selected the quotes at the end of each point to add more spice to the script and draw a correlation with 'more renowned' experts and distinguished persons. However, the quotes have been added at the end of writing the book to strengthen my point of view and not the other way around. To the best of my knowledge, the quotes do not infringe on any intellectual property issue.

I hope you will find the book interesting and it will add value to your existing or potential entrepreneurial journey.

Thanks
Md. Mubir M. Chowdhury
mubirc@gmail.com
LinkedIn: https://www.linkedin.com/in/mubir/

EDITOR'S NOTE

This is a well-timed book for the millennials cruising the startup ecosystem. Entrepreneurship takes more than insight. This book takes the reader through the planning phase, seed phase and growth phase just like a mentor by your side.

The Ideal Quitter wraps up a range of aspects, and myriad of challenges faced by entrepreneurs everywhere. This book will serve as a roadmap to foresee what is to come along the way and what pitfalls to slide past. Luck is nothing but being prepared for the opportunity; moreover, creating opportunities in the role of an entrepreneur. You will see how in the context of Bangladesh an entrepreneur's battle and win may look like, but the content is applicable for a general and worldwide audience. The style of this book is remarkable, segmented, with quotes from notable businessmen and timeless personalities adding up a unique layer!

The future CEOs will surely find a sleek overview on organizational management and leadership from this book.

I have worked in leading roles in companies like SEMAC, the Bangladesh wing of 10:10 Climate Action, ICCCAD and lastly my own startup nLight Design and I would keep *The Ideal Quitter* in my pocket.

Ishita Mouri Rahman
Editor
ishitarahman@hotmail.com

CONTENTS

Planning Phase 10

1. Remember: Every rose has its thorn 11
2. Entrepreneurship is still not well accepted in many cultures 13
3. Plan hard 15
4. Entrepreneurship is not 'cool' without available cash in your pocket 17
5. Plan ahead with family expenditure 18
6. Define your success criteria 19
7. Leave the first 7/15 days for family only 21
8. Don't go for every opportunity, Prioritize 22
9. Capitalize on your strength areas first 27
10. Identify a real problem to solve 29
11. An idea need not be 'cool', but effective 30
12. You don't need to 'reinvent the wheel' 32
13. Your product is only 10% of your business 35
14. Set your company vision, and be committed to it ... 38
15. Have the MVP (Minimum Viable Product) roadmap chalked out 39
16. Have a clear monetization plan 40
17. Business plan and Budgeting are necessary 42
18. A cash flow plan is extremely crucial 44
19. Check the financial viability of your idea 45

20. Generate clear idea on how to fill in the gaps of 'road to success' 47

21. Take good business partner(s) 49

Seed phase 53

22. Hire based on potential, not entirely on skill 54
23. Invest in good HR 56
24. Develop resources 58
25. Hire fast, fire fast: 59
26. Outsource works to able people 62
27. Create the MVP and hit the market ASAP 64
28. Perfection costs too much; improve as you grow ... 66
29. Focus more on effectiveness than on efficiency 68
30. Delegate to able resources 70
31. Get involved in short term cash generation 71
32. Do not get engaged in more than two activities 73
33. Minimize fixed cost and overhead 75
34. Let go of your ego 79
35. Ask for help with caution 82
36. Beware of opportunists inside your close circle 85
37. Trust everyone with due diligence 87
38. You are the whole value chain of your office 89
39. Don't be afraid to make mistakes; however, don't repeat the mistakes 91
40. Be proactive and future-ready 93
41. Make sure to keep your commitment 95

42. Legal documentation is boring but very critical for growth 97

43. Maintain your business accounts from the very beginning 99

44. Plan well ahead to maintain a positive cash flow . 101

45. Don't fall in love with your product 103

46. Know when to drop your product, and move to the next one 106

47. Onboard investors very cautiously........................ 109

48. It might be a double-edged sword to get funded early 111

49. Awards are good, but revenue is best 114

50. Minimize cost, maximize investment.................... 117

51. Your own salary is nothing but a number 119

Growth Phase 121

52. Get involved in critical activities, let employees do the rest 122

53. Engage the employees with your vision 124

54. Treat your employees so well that they love you . 126

55. Accept that you are a stepping stone for a better future for your employees.................................... 127

56. Cost estimation will overshoot, but revenue target will fail 130

57. Raising capital for your business is not a success, making it profitable is:... 131

58. Create strategic partnership for value generation 134

59. Keep the focus on the big picture 136

60. Concentrate on and celebrate short, mid, and long-term success.. 137

61. Focus on sustainable revenue: 139

62. Getting a bit late success is okay 141

Overall Direction.. 144

63. Don't waste resources; it's too scarce for a startup 145

64. Have a dream so large that won't let you quit 147

65. Keep 'exit' options limited: 149

66. It's not a 100-meter sprint, rather a marathon 151

67. Patience is critical 153

68. Money is very important, but you need a bigger motivation 156

69. The higher you were, the harder will be the adjustment 158

70. You can't get a business up with a full stomach 161

71. Commit time in additional businesses with caution: 163

72. Family is everything; deprive them within limit 166

73. Be Positive and don't look back 169

74. Don't let the negativity of other people dampen your energy 171

75. Luck is a major factor 173

76. Be passionate 175

77. Push to the end, but know when to quit 177

78. **Keep praying to the Almighty** 178

Conclusion 180

Bonus part 181

  Ten signs that you will be an early quitting entrepreneur 182

Reference 186

Planning Phase

1. Remember: Every rose has its thorn

We hear the success stories of entrepreneurs and their world-changing efforts. Little do we know about how much pain they had to endure to reach this point! Digesting failures and going through this journey is not for the faintest of hearts.

In the first four years, there were at least four incidents when I had almost given up. I was close to putting an end to my dream by getting back to a job with a fixed income. I could not further take financial pressure and uncertainty. However, till now I have been able to manage the obstacles and go on pursuing my dream to become a fruitful entrepreneur. Although I have grown older in this journey, the struggle persists.

In 2013, I and 167 colleagues of my former employer quit our jobs and availed a voluntary retirement scheme. Around 60 of them embarked on the path of entrepreneurship to catch their dreams. After four years (in 2017), only three to four members including me were still fighting in the entrepreneurial field. The rest gave up and rejoined jobs or migrated to other countries in search of a better life.

The financial woes coupled with stress may at times become too much to take by anyone, especially those who are not on the top of their game. It demands patience to carry on and see it till the end. There will be extreme cases where you will doubt your ability and fail to get the expected output e.g. your expected quarterly cash flow. Such times would quite drain you out of your energy to fight further. Even though the struggle sounds very romantic and dramatic, these experiences create a morale shattering impact. Knowing about the pain is not enough to grasp the bitterness of the phase until they really happen to you.

No one can sense the hollow feeling of becoming virtually bankrupt unless you become one. No one can prepare you to look at the eyes of your employees and say that their salaries will be 'further delayed' when the previous month's salary is still pending. It will be an immense psychological pressure to perform right so that you can sleep well at night.

As an entrepreneur or an aspiring one, you have to dream big and look towards becoming successful. Yet keep in mind that to reach success, you need to cross a great sea of bitterness where at any point you might lose the motivation to move ahead any further and give up.

Relevant quote:

Unknown: "Everyone wants to be successful until they see what it takes."

2. Entrepreneurship is still not well accepted in many cultures

Dropping a college degree or quitting a job to follow your dreams to become an entrepreneur may seem meaningful in the developed economies while it is the opposite in developing and underdeveloped economies. Weighing greater value on financial security in present tense trumps overtaking risk to gain something much bigger in the future. Everyone appreciates entrepreneurship and knows that it may be the biggest scope to acquire wealth until it is taken up by someone close in the family. The primary reason is the lack of any social security net to pull up anyone whose financial condition has nose-dived while exploring an entrepreneurial dream.

In weaker economies, it is tough to run your own business and manage the required funds. This sums up to a higher probability of failure to your entrepreneurship compared to a similar endeavor in a stronger economy. The governments in the latter are ready to catch you if you fall. The entrepreneurial eco-system is also much seasoned where investors have more confidence to invest in your business.

Whether or not you belong to such a 'lesser privileged' economy or a 'privileged' one, you have to first get the buy-in of your immediate family members (especially your dependents) before taking such a huge decision as their standard of living might be impacted by your decision. They need to grasp that the so far 'for-granted' things (e.g. those regular dine-outs, that once in a year holiday trip etc.) will not be that regular anymore. Most likely there will be a direct impact on how you are planning your family budget (e.g. that good school you want your child to get into, but now it's out of your reach etc.).

Failure to get their buy-in may result in a huge internal pressure to get back to a job as they will not share your spirit and judge you differently. Yet your social circle might still consider you crazy and keep a keen eye on your performance.

In a developing country's scenario, as an early level entrepreneur, you have to be ready to face social judgment on your decision-making capabilities. By default, you will be considered a 'lost cause'. You will know that the near and dear ones are talking behind your back about 'what a big mistake' you have made by not pursuing a steady job! As a cherry on top of the cake, if you are a guy who is yet to get married, you might find it pretty difficult to get your favorite girl's parents' permission. They will not be eager to get their daughter married to someone whose success is not at all visible, and social status not up to the mark like an employee of a renowned organization.

Relevant quote:

Jeff Bezos (American technology entrepreneur, investor, and philanthropist. He is the founder, chairman, and chief executive officer of Amazon): "Entrepreneurs must be willing to be misunderstood for long periods!"

3. Plan hard

It's very easy to turn into an entrepreneur; but rather difficult to become a successful one. To be successful, you need to plan deep; for both short and long-term success. Don't just decide to become an entrepreneur on a bad day at work, and quit right away. Instead, take your time to find the right idea that has clear potential in the market. Preferably, do the dry run while you are still on the job. If you find the idea potent enough, then and only then, quit the job. It might help to save up at least six months of your entrepreneurial time that would have to be run without any fixed income.

The first place where entrepreneurs fail to plan is to estimate the time and money required as a capital investment to build the 'machine' to get the vital output. They also fail to plan on how to manage the working capital to run the company until sufficient revenue is achieved. In between, there are many other smaller but very important matters where failure to plan will result in significant loss of effectiveness and efficiency.

However, also never think that you will quit when the new venture's income will somewhat get near to your current income. It will never happen! A smart company only employs a new person when the position is justified with its cost-benefit ratio. This concludes that there is a certain reason that your company is paying you and that's because it requires a person's whole day's productive work to do it. So, it is highly unlikely that you will be able to put the required effort to make your venture fly high by working in the off-hours and weekends only.

Yes, you can make the basic structure at that time. Although to make it big and profitable within a considerable time, you need to invest a lot of your productive time in developing, managing, marketing, and selling your product/service for and to the customers. You can take two routes. One would be to keep your job and run your business as a side income source where it never becomes your top priority. The second would be to make your venture your top priority by quitting your existing job and go for an all-out effort to make it successful. You must remember that you can create a business very easily, but to make it sustainable you need to invest in it. By the word 'investment', I mean both your time and money!

At the end of the day, it has to be a leap of faith. You need to make an inner call! You can compare your existing job's ROI (return on investment) with that of the possible ROI of your new venture. You go for your venture only when your calculation predicts a better future return. However, I would like to emphasize on the definition of success once again as a quotient where the ROI does not necessarily have to be in monetary form. It can also come in the form of 'peace of mind' or 'working on your passion'. It may come from self-actualization and non-financial achievement too.

As for me, failure to plan in the early part of my entrepreneur journey has cost me at least a year's investment which I consider as 'learning cost'. These funds just flew away before properly understanding what I want. Interestingly it took me about another year to ascertain how I want it! And I am still learning…

Relevant quote:

Benjamin Franklin (Founding Father of the United States): "By failing to prepare, you are preparing to fail."

4. Entrepreneurship is not 'cool' without available cash in your pocket

In the current age of social media, I quite frequently see 20 somethings as CEOs in their own companies. I am truly not sure whether these people are doing any good by becoming 'CEO's so early on in their career. I don't have any negativity about being a young CEO, but I express my concern over the fact that to be successful in running a company you need to have a certain amount of maturity. Failing to run a company in a profitable manner will only result in losing a few precious years (and a good amount of your investors' money). You may lose the most energetic time of your career if you can't run a great game.

With the help of different programs and incubators, and the colorful stories spreading over the internet, people have access to more information than ever about entrepreneurship. Yet, to my concern, I am seeing that only the rose tainted pictures are being portrayed. Words like 'hard work' and 'perseverance' come in a very shallow manner failing (to say the least) to convey the right level of hardship to come on the way to success. Entrepreneurship becomes a cool thing to do, through which you achieve your dreams with 'hard work'!

This coolness and initial enthusiasm hit the brick wall when you start to pay from your pocket for the employees' salaries and other fixed expenses. Soon enough, the coolness dries out and gets replaced with fear of failure and uncertainty if you continue on this path. Strikingly, no startup incubator or talk show will prepare you for that! Unless you already have an angel investor or VC in sight; you might already be swimming in hot soup with a rise in debts and pressure on personal accounts at the end of every month.

Relevant quote:

Thomas Jefferson (American Founding Father who was the principal author of the Declaration of Independence and later served as the third President of the United States from 1801 to 1809): "Never spend your money before you have earned it."

5. Plan ahead with family expenditure

Every person has their view of how much money is required to sustain their family and maintain a minimum standard of living. With that in mind, you need to make your family budget very early on your entrepreneurial journey. With no fixed monthly income in hand, you need to have a clear forecast of how much you can spend on family matters. The last thing you want is an empty pocket with bills to pay at the end of the month. Thus, you have to allocate some money in your account to pull you through the non-productive period (if possible, money for a year or more). This is the time when your business will not generate any profit to plow back into running your home.

Ideally, to cope up in the uncertain days to come, you should put an average of a year's reserve for your family expenses. This amount should reflect on the bare minimum amount required to sustain your standard of living. This fund should be stripped off any additional or luxury expenses like going on a vacation, getting a new car, or redecorating the house, etc.

Nonetheless cutting too much on your family expenses could impact your standard of living and result in losing morale and a very critical support of your spouse, kids and other important family members!

Relevant quote:

Warren Buffett (American business magnate, investor, speaker, and philanthropist): "Do not save what is left after spending, but spend what is left after saving!"

6. Define your success criteria

Many a time, when I asked my young trainees (I am also a soft skills trainer; particularly in the field of customer experience management, customer service, B2B sales, and business communication), who are mostly university students or fresh graduates, about their 'aim in life'. In 99% cases I find very shallow answers like "to be a businessman", or "to get a good salaried job". Unfortunately, these are merely steps in life and can never be termed as destinations. From that perspective, I have formed an opinion that people (irrespective of age - very young, young, or middle-aged) are highly confused about what to achieve in their life. They are not sure how to make their life 'successful'. To most, success is earning money, a lot of it, and that's all. In my opinion, earning enough money is a milestone and can hardly be termed as a pure success criterion. Everybody wants to earn sufficient money. It is more important to clearly understand what you want to do with the money.

'Success' is a very vague word, to say the least, and is a very relative matter. Your definition of success today may be dwarfed if you compare it with tomorrow's one; or even worse, compare it with other's success. So, it's important that you define your success criteria, or at least have a clear idea about it, before leaping into the entrepreneurial world. To some, success may be earning tons of money and fly personally owned chopper. To others, success might be to become their own boss and leading a modest yet respectful life. Yet, for some, success might mean to get involved in self-actualizing missions like helping the under-privileged. Hence, you have to decide on your end goal and your venture should be a vehicle to drive you there. It can be applied to your life too, even if you want to pursue your career by not becoming an entrepreneur as well.

If you are unsure about your definition of success, it's utterly likely that you will get diverted on the way. You might find yourself chasing auxiliary matters, putting aside the primary success criteria. It's also likely that you will lose the interest to pursue a continuous uphill climb and stop on your tracks when finding it too difficult. The lack of knowing the proper motivating factor to chase, can be draining.

Relevant quote:

Robert Louis Stevenson (Scottish novelist and travel writer, most noted for Treasure Island, Kidnapped, Strange Case of Dr. Jekyll and Mr. Hyde, and A Child's Garden of Verses): "An aim in life is the only fortune worth finding."

7. Leave the first 7/15 days for family only

You have to understand and acknowledge that the entrepreneurship journey that you have opted to pursue will require a lot of your waking hours - all of your working time and some of your personal time. You have decided to be your own boss and whatever you do, you will do it for yourself. No matter how motivating that sounds, the fact of the matter is that you now have more responsibilities in your hand. It's the responsibility to bring up a toddler and make it healthy and matured enough to take care of itself. This nurturing from childhood to maturity takes a lot of time, energy and resources. No matter how hard you try, it is highly unlikely that it will happen within a short time.

Most of the job quitting entrepreneurs fail to understand it and think that 'everything will be fine' within the next six months or so. I made the same mistake and withheld my family vacation for the days when 'things will start to get smooth' and I will be drawing a regular salary from my business. Interestingly, it took me more than five years to have the first family vacation since I started my business.

So, if you have decided to quit, submitted your resignation, and passed the last day at work; my strong suggestion will be to unwind yourself and pass some quality time with your family. Depending on the weight of your pocket, you can go for a small vacation or outing with your family members. Once you start your new entrepreneurial journey, you will cherish this small vacation!

Relevant quote:

Unknown: "No amount of money or success can take the place of time spent with your family."

8. Don't go for every opportunity, Prioritize

After you quit the job and start working on the opportunities, a whole horizon of them will open up to you, virtually from every direction. A friend might call you up to drive his 'great idea.' Some news of opportunity might arrive while having a chat with someone else. Don't go for every money-making idea that you come across.

You have to analyze and measure your grasp of the domain knowledge and ROI (Return on Investment) or value (benefit divided by cost) from that business. Once you get a hold of it, it will be easier for you to decide which opportunity to follow. You have to remember that each time you pursue (or at least explore) a certain endeavor, it will involve certain time, energy, and other resources which are your investment. Failure to ascertain the ROI or the returning value will lead to a loss in investment and missing out on other more feasible projects.

Nonetheless, it is logical that you will keep a short list of opportunities at the initial stage (I had 8, to start with). However, you need to shorten the list to 1 or 2 within a few weeks' (at max months) time upon proper analysis. Finally, choose the one(s) with the highest ROI or value.

The main challenge to prioritize ideas in this phase is the lack of information in your hand. Thus, going for detailed business plan, calculating ROIs, and prioritizing based on that will most probably be not possible. The next best thing to do will be to calculate the 'Business Potential Analysis'. I initially got the idea from a writeup from 'entrepreneurship in a box' [7] and then I modified it according to my liking.

Considering that right now you don't have sufficient data to execute detailed analysis and go deep into the subject matter; you can do a shallow analysis with your available assumptions. In this analysis, you take into consideration a few factors like your domain knowledge, level of existing competition, potential to monetize the idea, profitability, size of the market, and initial investment requirement. You can also add factors like entry barrier, market sophistication etc. Add your own factors or delete from the above lists as you see fit for your endeavor.

Firstly, you put the business ideas available at hand on one axis of a matrix, and place the factors in another. Then place marks from for each factor against every business idea. You can also put a weight for the factors to fine tune your prioritized areas. You then multiply the weight with the received mark against the factors under each business idea banner and add the results together. You should pick the business idea that comes out with the highest mark.

Sounds complicated? Not at all. Just let me give you an example. Suppose you have two ideas in hand and you're not sure which one to pursue. You decide to do a business potential analysis. You take the six factors mentioned above and place them in the following table:

	Factors	Weight	Idea 1	Idea 2
1.	My domain knowledge			
2.	Level of existing competition			
3.	Potential to monetize the idea			
4.	Profitability			
5.	Size of the market			
6.	Initial investment requirement			

Then, you start to put the weight in % terms against each factor depending on the relevant importance you feel against each factor. To remain factor neutral for all the above six, you can place 16.67% weight for each of the factors if you think all of them are equally important. However, depending on your domain knowledge you might prefer to explore mass market ideas or niche market ideas. If you go for mass market ideas, then there is a higher possibility that there is already competition here and thus the idea has potentially lower profitability. Just in case, you want to put more emphasis on profitability, then place a higher weight on the factor and move accordingly.

So, after putting equal weight, the table now looks like this:

THE IDEAL QUITTER

Factors	Weight	Idea 1	Idea 2
1. My domain knowledge	16.67%		
2. Level of existing competition	16.67%		
3. Potential to monetize the idea	16.67%		
4. Profitability	16.67%		
5. Size of the market	16.67%		
6. Initial investment requirement	16.67%		

Then you start putting marks against each of the factors for both the ideas. Here you have to remember that you put higher mark for favorable situation and lower mark for non-favorable situation. For example, if the initial investment is higher and you are short in that capacity, a higher investment requirement will be a non-favorable situation and thus will receive a lower mark. You can set the marking the following manner:

Very unfavorable	Unfavorable	Neutral	Favorable	Very favorable
1	3	5	7	9

Thus, if you analyze the above two business ideas and find that idea 1 requires significantly higher initial investment (very high than your capacity) than idea 2, which you can comfortably manage. Then you can put 1 and 9 against idea 1 and 2 for 'initial investment' factor. You have to place the relevant marks for each factor and come up with a filled in table like the following:

Factors	Weight	Idea 1	Idea 2
1. My domain knowledge (Rationale: I don't have much knowledge on Idea 1; whereas, I am kind of an expert in Idea 2 field)	16.67%	3	7
2. Level of existing competition (Rationale: the market for Idea 1 is already very competitive with already a number of players in the field, whereas Idea 2 has very low or no competition)	16.67%	3	9

Factors	Weight	Idea 1	Idea 2
3. Potential to monetize the idea (Rationale: Idea 1 already has a proven monetization potential than its counterpart)	16.67%	7	3
4. Profitability (Rationale: Due to relatively higher competition, Idea 1 already is approaching a market saturation, and thus profit is shirking fast; on the other hand even with a moderate competition, the competition is still not very structured and I can bring out some good profit from it)	16.67%	3	9
5. Size of the market (Rationale: Idea 1 has a much larger market, whereas Idea 2 has a niche market)	16.67%	9	1
6. Initial investment requirement (Rationale: The required investment for Idea 1 is extremely difficult for me to manage, where I can start Idea 2 with almost no initial investment)	16.67%	1	9

After giving scores, you need to multiply the scores with the weight and will get an absolute score. After adding relevant scores for all the factors under each product, you will get the business potential score for each idea as per your own preference. The final table should look like this:

Factors		Weight	Idea 1		Idea 2	
			Relevant score	Total score	Relevant score	Total score
1.	My domain knowledge	16.67%	3	0.50	7	1.17
2.	Level of existing competition	16.67%	3	0.50	9	1.50
3.	Potential to monetize the idea	16.67%	7	1.17	3	0.50
4.	Profitability	16.67%	3	0.50	9	1.50
5.	Size of the market	16.67%	9	1.50	1	0.17
6.	Initial investment requirement	16.67%	1	0.17	9	1.50
Total Business Potential Score				4.51		7.51

So, here Idea 2 is a clear winner and you should decide to move ahead with it by scrapping Idea 1 from your list. You have to make sure that no matter how many tests you run in this model; the weights and marking standards have to remain consistent. You should keep the weights fixed for a certain time based on your own capacity and business preferences. Here you have to remain clear to yourself that you will put weights and relevant marks against each of the factors for their true value, not because you want a certain idea to win. In such a case, you don't need to run the business potential analysis in the first place!

Relevant quote:

Stephen Covey (American educator, author, businessman, and keynote speaker): "The key is not to prioritize what's on your schedule but to schedule your priorities."

9. Capitalize on your strength areas first

While you explore a particular opportunity, it is very important to have your hold on it. I highly discourage anyone to venture into a completely unknown field, just because it is profitable. Each industry has its own culture, norms, and practices that you need to accustom to before investing in it. By putting money in an industry before grasping its 'language', you are almost certain to incur some losses (I rather call it 'learning expenses'). You may also get your fingers burnt before starting to understand. I lost a quarter of my savings within a few months by trying to do business in the ready-made garments industry, albeit having fewer ideas. However, I jumped in motivated by success stories worth millions of dollars and getting filthy rich just within a few years of operations. The good part is that I soon jumped off the wagon right when I knew that my entire savings are not enough to sustain me up to the point where I can make profit.

So instead of following the success stories, let's first try to see if you can create some scope within your knowledge domain. For example, if you are a banker, consider creating a banking process automation tool that is not available in the market right now. Then market it in the relevant segment where you know the decision-makers to make some quick breakthrough. The best part is that you know what you are getting into as a subject matter expert. Otherwise, you run the risk of making some costly mistakes that might break your morale and financial backbone.

In my job life, I worked at B2B sales department as a Key Account Manager to sell telecom products to corporate entities. At a later stage I also worked at the customer experience management department. Here I worked in a strategic unit to improve the overall customer loyalty with the brand. Then I finally co-founded and settled in with two ventures among which both are in my somewhat known domain. One is a training and consultancy firm where I work with my clients to improve the customer experience of their brand. The second is a software development firm where I am developing products to automate business processes which I had the opportunity to explore while I worked in B2B sales.

Relevant quote:

Steve Maraboli (life-changing Speaker, bestselling Author, and Behavioral Scientist): Accept yourself, your strengths, your weaknesses, your truths, and know what tools you have to fulfill your purpose.

10. Identify a real problem to solve

This is one of the most crucial areas to work on at the very early stage of your entrepreneurship. Your startup will emerge on the very notion of the outcome of this thought process. A business makes money by solving real-life problems; and your job is to brainstorm and identify that real problem. Every available solution in the market (be it a product or a service) solves a problem; may it be saving effort, money, or time. For example, Uber reduces the stress of customers to find a transport, Airbnb helps customers to find good accommodation at an economy rate, etc. One technique is to look around your society and come up with a burning issue to solve. You can look at your domain of work and find out the inefficiency in it that you want to solve.

The problem found needs a solution for which your potential customers are willing to pay enough. You can target mass market problems, or problems to solve niche market issues. To test the opportunity concept, you can do some quick market testing by drawing in people from the relevant market segment. You can ask different questions to identify the magnitude of the problem in their lives and how much they are willing to pay to get a solution.

However, there is always a chance that you will be brainstorming innovative solutions to a latent demand, which is not at all considered a problem right now. For instance, what sort of market study would tell you the potential of Facebook before it was born? For game-changing innovations, there is no alternative but to create an MVP (Minimum Viable Product) and to test them in the market to watch the customers' reactions.

Relevant quote:

Albert Einstein (German-born theoretical physicist who developed the theory of relativity, one of the two pillars of modern physics): "No problem can be solved with the same level of consciousness that created it."

11. An idea need not be 'cool', but effective

We are facing a terrible challenge living in the social media era. We like to brag about ourselves and consider how others will like our ideas with a 'like', 'wow', and 'love' react on Facebook. We tend to be attracted to fancy and fluffy ideas that will create WOW instantly. The cooler the idea, the bigger the number of 'likes' are. Certainly, that's not a problem, unless you are fixated on the 'coolness' of the idea rather than your thought on solving the actual problem. The business feasibility is the biggest question after all!

Consider the case of 'Dabbawala' in India, the legendary food transportation system that delivers hot lunches from homes and restaurants to people at work in India, especially in Mumbai. Although it is a homely service executed by mostly simple people in a very analog manner; it is considered a Six Sigma level organization in terms of efficiency [1].

What would you do if you find an issue like that of 'Dabbawala' to solve? It may not be as much gorgeous to work on and will deal with regular day to day life of common people. It will be messy and in short, not be typically 'cool'. On the other hand, more laudable issues like global warming or gender equality may get more attention. However, winning admiration and creating a sustainable business are two completely different matters.

My IT company developed two applications; both of which were generated from real-life challenges. The first one, Madviser, helped to reduce the mobile communication expense of individual users. The other one, Selliscope, helped distribution-based sales organizations to bring more efficiency to their sales channel by reducing paper cost and reporting time.

We sensed the need for an app like 'Madviser' within a week of quitting our jobs when our mobile phones were barred for crossing the credit limit. The primary reason for this was not being in the right package and getting charged excessively. Previously we enjoyed an uninterrupted calling facility, being a member of a mobile telecom organization. We tested the first MVP and it was an instant hit. With the expense of only USD 150 worth promotion on Facebook (followed by some favorable media attention), the app was downloaded approx. 15,000 times within 1 month. It was the proof of the concept that we were looking for. Nonetheless, we had to put the project into a freezer for having a low marketing budget and it lacked the response expected from investors as it was a long shot game.

Whereas the proof of concept for a product like 'Selliscope' was already there. As I mentioned earlier, I worked at a B2B Sales team with my previous employer and dealt with a few sales driven organizations. There I saw the pitfalls in the customers' lives and how they were trying to solve the challenges with low tech yet expensive solutions. There was a clear scope of improving their working process using better technology. Hence, after forming the company when we came across one such similar opportunity asked by one client, we did not hesitate to pursue it. In the process, we developed 'Selliscope' (now re-branded as 'Sokrio')

Relevant quote:

Napoleon Hill (American author, known best for his book 'Think and Grow Rich'): "Your big opportunity may be right where you are now"

12. You don't need to 'reinvent the wheel'

First of all, let me brief the concept of 'reinventing the wheel'. It means to go through the whole learning process and do the trial and error part to accomplish something that someone has already done before. The 'wheel' is one of the most significant inventions of mankind that contributed to a dramatic improvement in communication. It revolutionized the transport of goods and people. Even though seemingly a very simple idea, the first person to carved a piece of stone or wood might have taken years to come up with. Most likely it was a long process of trial and error with varying shapes and ingredients. Once the first wheel was invented, it would be a complete waste of time, energy and resource to reinvent the wheel. The smart approach would be to research the existing wheel and improve on its features to add some value to it.

To many people, entrepreneurship sounds like an all-out innovation and doing things that are completely new in the domain. This notion is half true in the sense that you as an entrepreneur, need to learn from others' innovations and then set your business by adding some value to it. If you want to start from scratch, it would cost you much more time and resources to learn what others have already learned before. Practically all you need to do is to observe the competitors, similar products, developments and analyze them followed by brainstorming to add some value to the already developed product.

The vital matter is that it must solve a new challenge or an existing challenge in a better way. Even then, you might need to develop the product from the very beginning, but at least you know what you are building at the start of your planning phase. A true inventor does not necessarily know what the outcome might look like; and hence need to spend a lot of resources in research and development.

In the current era, once you identify your working area, you can browse through relevant internet sites to know customer reviews on the existing products in the market. This will yield you the improvement areas. You can even buy your competitor's products to gain consumer experience and find where they are lacking. You can get primary data through formal market research to know your market and competitors ahead of time before launching a product.

You can also take a solution from a market and apply it in another market with necessary customizations/ innovations. For instance, it's a very common practice that technologies are transferred from one country to another. Different hardware and software are developed based on ideas taken from other countries or industries. The easiest way to introduce a new product or service is to find a challenge to solve in your market first and find the solutions of the same challenge in other countries/ markets. Take the idea of the solution, apply it directly if it fits right into your challenge or customize it for your country or market's scenario. The rest depends on how you execute the solution in your target market.

'Uber' revolutionized the concept of ride-sharing and has been identified as one of the hottest startups in the world. In Bangladesh, 'Pathao' took Uber's idea and introduced a ride-sharing app as well. Notably, Both Uber and Pathao launched their ride-sharing services in Bangladesh within a month's gap in late 2016. The twist in Pathao's approach was it launched with sharing of motorbikes instead of cars catering to the needs of Dhaka city, known for its bumper to bumper jam. It was an instant hit as it solved the city dwellers challenge to reach their destination on time. This idea stirred the market so much that Uber had to change their approach and include bike-sharing along with its traditional car-sharing (launched Uber Moto in 2017). However, it took Uber around one year to make this move while Pathao had already established a strong foothold in the market. If Pathao launched with car sharing, it would be just a 'me too' product like Uber. As a result, Pathao would lose its critical advantage over its world champion competitor. Interestingly enough, Pathao was not the first motorbike sharing app in Bangladesh, rather it was 'SAM'. It launched its service around five months even before Pathao, yet it could not grab the market due to inferior execution and business model. [2]

Relevant quote:

Mark Hume McCormack (American lawyer, sports agent, writer, founder and chairman of International Management Group, now

IMG): "You don't have to reinvent the wheel, just attach it to a new wagon."

13. Your product is only 10% of your business

It's needless to say that to have a successful business, you must have a good product. By the term 'good' I mean that the product should solve the intended challenge, and preferably surpass anyone else. Without a good product, it's very unlikely that you will be able to generate sustainable business out of it.

Having a good product in hand does not vitally ensure a good business. Quite often the people around me come up with different problems in life and ask me to develop IT solutions in hope of a quick fix. In every case, I candidly refuse these offers as a product in itself takes quite a lot of resources to develop. Then it takes even more to market, sell, manage, and finally make some profit out of it.

To generate a successful business, apart from having a good product team, you need to maintain a balanced team of sales, marketing, HR, admin, finance, and other relevant people to carry out the business. Quite often, an early-stage entrepreneur somewhat misses out the importance of planning for the other functions. In my opinion, this mistake can be the result of inexperience or over-enthusiasm for the intended product-market fit. The entrepreneur becomes overconfident with his or her anticipated 'sure-shot' business immediately after the MVP (minimum viable product) is launched. A very common mistake an early-stage entrepreneur makes is he or she fails to foresee what will happen after the MVP (minimum viable product) is made.

In most cases, as an entrepreneur, you will maintain strong attention and focus on developing the product. You will tend to forego the thought of successfully marketing and selling the product to the intended target market (when it reaches a sellable level). Here, the entrepreneur keeps the provision of just enough funds in hand to develop the product only. That too considering that everything will go as planned and the 'perfect' and 'bug-free' product will be developed at the first attempt. He or she hopes that sales and marketing will be 'somehow managed' eventually. It's even more common to forego the thoughts of the administrative aspects where you forget to take into account the cost of management. Also, the cost of ongoing product development along with the continuation of company operations and legal costs are overlooked. As a result of missing out on crucial aspects of your business, you may fail to include them in your budget.

In my opinion, the terrible lapse in the planning phase is one of the key root causes of startup failures. The reason the startup fails is that it runs out of cash to meet its operational cost. As an entrepreneur, overlooking costs will put huge pressure on your operations. You will always be under pressure to manage the funds to meet your ongoing expenses.

Even if you start with a deep pocket and have sufficient provision for sales, marketing, and other stuff, you will fumble without a thorough business continuity model. The product alone cannot save you from going out of business. Success demands diligent planning and execute operations to attract buyers. The chain completes by selling the product to your target market and ensuring a good service along with your product.

Let me get back to the original header of this section about the product being only 10% of the business! Why do I think like that? Many effective products have failed to business successfully purely for the failure in operations. Even if the product is of a satisfactory level, you can jeopardize your business by failing to plan and execute. If you expect that your product will be so 'great' that people will automatically come in flocks and purchase your product; then I have to say that most likely you are living in a fool's world!

Just for further demonstration in line with the example given in the last chapter, I can mention about the motorcycle ride-sharing service 'SAM (Share A Motorcycle)' in Bangladesh. Even though it launched the service a few months earlier than its competitors 'Pathao' and 'Uber', it failed to create a successful business. The failure primarily took place because of its faulty operations management and poor revenue sharing model that was not attractive enough to its 'riders' (the motorcycle service providers). Even though it had the first-mover advantage, yet it failed to market this product and get significant downloads, create a good user base, and become one of the leading players. I am sure, the management of SAM thought of introducing a super disruptive product in the market that people will welcome with wide hands. They were expecting to get a natural pull from both service providers and users! So, SAM could not do well in the market not because it had a faulty product, but more for poor strategy and execution. [2]

Relevant quote:

Eric McFadden (American guitarist, vocalist, and songwriter): "If you want people to buy your products, your products have to become a part of their environment."

14. Set your company vision, and be committed to it

The company vision is the dream that you want your organization to transform into. It indicates what sort of impact you want to make with your business. Vision has to convey a clear picture of the company's future and your ambition should reflect through it. There is a saying, "*If you are not scared after setting it, and people do not call you crazy; then you are yet to set the right vision!*"

Microsoft Corporation's vision statement is "to help individuals and businesses realize their full potential". The company that started as a pure software company, plays a role in combining individuals and businesses to achieve full potential. It is a daunting task for them, even at this stage. It requires a lot of planning, execution, market feedback and stumbles to achieve the vision. This vision will drive them to become better and better all through their operations.

You may start your business in your living room but must set your dream on what you want to become. That dream certainly will be a far-fetched one. Sitting here right now, it's not at all possible to predict whether your company will be able to achieve it or not. Yet, you need to set the dream, the vision. Setting a proper vision helps you to keep track of your development and avoid distractions on the way.

The vision is my guiding principle behind my works. In my case, me and my partners decided to pursue our dream to *"become a world-renowned innovation-driven digital solutions provider through delivering excellent customer experience"*. The interesting part is that we did not even have our own office when we set our dream to become a top company in the world. Even after five years of operations, I won't even dare to say that I have come any close to that dream with my company.

Relevant quote:

Unknown: "Remember why you started."

15. Have the MVP (Minimum Viable Product) roadmap chalked out

MVP or the Minimum Viable Product is the first commercial version of a product that can be used for its intended purpose with the minimum acceptable features in it. No matter how much concept testing you have done, it all boils down to this point. Here people use your product on a serious note to achieve a certain purpose and preferably on payment. MVP is the acid test that will give you a good idea of the feasibility and marketability of your product. It will also indicate how you need to design the actual product in the post MVP stage if it becomes successful.

MVP mainly serves the purpose of getting direct customer feedback on the features and usability. It also ascertains the viable amount to be paid by customers for the service. If you do not overdo the features or delay your MVP launch, it brings out the hard facts from customer's mind and generates high-quality insight for the product or service provider. It helps the startup to make the way forward efficient and minimize rework on further features based on customer demand. The earlier customer(s) start adopting the MVP and actively contribute feedback in the development process of the product, the better it is.

A successfully launched MVP will save you a lot of money, effort, and market research as you will get feedback directly from the customers on the next requirements. All you need is to prioritize which features to build next and arrange money for the development and subsequent marketing.

Relevant quote:

Eric Ries (American entrepreneur, blogger, and author of The Lean Startup, a book on the lean startup movement): "Don't be in a rush to get big. Be in a rush to have a great product."

16. Have a clear monetization plan

No matter how brilliant your idea is, you need to earn sufficient money to sustain your business. Quite sometimes, brilliant and super cool ideas fail because they fail to monetize their product. Having a clear idea about how to monetize your startup is as crucial as identifying the timeline on when your startup will be able to start monetizing. Failing to identify how long it will take to monetize to reach a sustainable level and cover all the expenses might put your business at stake.

Unless you have a clear idea about the above matters, there is no doubt that you will end up in the middle of the road of product development with no money in hand. You will be on a lookout for investment from angel investors or VC firms or loans from financial institutions. This will not be an easy task to accomplish. It usually takes a minimum of 6 months of serious discussion to get an investor onboard whereas around 3 months to get a loan from a financial institution under favorable conditions. If you fail to manage it, you might have to end up salvaging your dream product. It will also cost you a lot of time and money with a bonus of digesting the stares from the unpaid staff.

Like I said, before you move ahead with your product idea, it is best to scope out the possible revenue streams from your product. There are certain ways that you can monetize your product/idea. Generally, tech startups generate revenue from their products from:
   a. Advertisements
   b. Agency-based activities like commissions from transactions made in their platform,
   c. Subscriptions fees if they develop a SaaS (Software as a Service) platform,
   d. One-time platform sales (like a generic software sold to a corporate customer)
   e. Data-based revenue is the most highly sought out where you sell consolidated insights generated from your product/software to the interested parties. Anyhow, it's a much-refined practice with controversy sometimes. Thus, think carefully before you venture into the data-based revenue stream.

You have to identify the best way to monetize your product right from the start. Don't blame others if you find yourself in a cash crunch in the middle of the development process.

Relevant quote:

Tara Hunt (Canadian author, speaker, and startup founder): "Designing your product for monetization first, and people second will probably leave you with neither."

17. Business plan and Budgeting are necessary

Even the seemingly best revenue earning ideas have their investment and OPEX needs. Good budgeting will save you from the uncertainty of getting broke. Budgeting is a plan on how you want to spend your money within a certain period. Budgeting helps to identify the cost sectors and generate a cumulative idea about the cost of total product/business development and management. Many startups crash purely for the failure of developing a good budget at the start of their journey.

To prepare a good budget, firstly you need to pinpoint the elements required to develop your product or service. For a product-based IT startup, the primary cost elements are the software engineers who will code and develop your software, and maintain the server where you will host your software, the graphics designers who will design the user interface and experience of the product and so on. At a later stage, you will need business development executives to drive revenue from the product. You will further need a product manager when the product will reach a minimum size. You might need a call center setup and agents to provide customer support. On top of that, there are marketing expenses, legal expenses, office costs, and relevant overheads like electricity bill, furniture expenses, etc. and the list goes on. What is striking is that a seemingly small idea with a low investment becomes a fairly large project once you add up all the components. Be realistic on the potential timeframe and resources required while developing the budget, until you foresee the business sustaining itself. Generally, a budget plan of 3 to 5 years will help you predict the hardships to come.

Another integral part of budgeting is to chalk up the expected revenue in place. This will give a glimpse projection on the profit-generating potential of the business. Now that you are certain of your product development and management cost, it's time to put the business plan together.

The business plan is to forecast how you want to earn your revenue. Based on your revenue projection, you need to strategize on how you want to push for the sale. The bigger the push the more resource you will need in the sales, support, and marketing team. This should also be reflected in the business plan. So, once you are done with the business plan and relevant budget, you will have a clear idea of how much money you are expected to generate from the revenue, the profit, and how much investment is required.

One of my ex-colleagues asked me if I was willing to be his partner in his new venture. By then he had already developed the beta version with his team and have started to approach potential customers. I became interested as the idea sounded exciting enough. However, once we developed the business plan and the budget accordingly, we found the business case is not feasible to pursue. Interestingly we invested only six working hours behind the business plan that saved us at least a year's hard work. Without the business plan, out of sheer positive feeling, we would have spent a lot of resources on developing the product and later find out that the market is not big enough for a sustainable business.

Relevant quote:

Dave Ramsey (American personal finance guru, businessman, and author): "A budget is telling your money where to go, instead of wondering where it went."

18. A cash flow plan is extremely crucial

It's okay to dream big, but you need to provide the necessary cash flow to the startup to make it work up till it generates sustainable revenue. First, you have to be clear on how you will monetize your idea, and finish preparing the budget along with the business plan. You should now be able to tell whether the business is motivating for you or not. Nonetheless, we are still missing one aspect, and that is the cash flow plan.

The cash flow statement helps you to identify the possible cash inflows and outflows. It comes up with a picture of the cash excess or shortage scenarios after a certain time frame (e.g. monthly, quarterly, half-yearly, yearly etc.). Based on that statement you can plan on how to finance the cash shortage period. A business can generate accounting profit, but can choke off its operations without the required cash flows. Many a time, your accounting profit might not be converted into cash just because the clients do not pay you on time; or some of your receivables become bad debts.

Cash flow statement formats are easily available on the internet. It's very easy to prepare a cash flow statement based on your expected realistic cash inflow and outflow projections. A good cash flow projection statement will give you a clear direction on how much money should you inject at a certain time. It will tell whether the generated cash from your own business will meet the demand; or in the best-case scenario, how much money you will be able to draw as a salary after quarter time.

Relevant quote:

Robert Kiyosaki (American businessman and author of 'Rich Dad Poor Dad'): "Making more money will not solve your problems if cash flow management is your problem."

19. Check the financial viability of your idea

Presumably, you have several ideas in hand. Logically you should invest in the most profitable one, or other words, the one with the most ROI (Return on Investment). It is paramount that you develop at least a 3 to 5-year business plan where both estimated cost and revenue will be plotted against each other. It will come up with a projected business performance picture for a certain period. The one with the largest ROI should prevail over the other ideas, and carried through.

Even so, developing this level of a business plan is quite time-consuming. It also requires a lot of attention to details that you might not have at the initial stage of an idea incubation. For the initial idea screening, you can choose simple impact estimation by talking to people near you. You can also estimate the level of engagement vis-a-vis the level of return against each other on a high level.

Nonetheless, I would recommend you to NOT take up any particular idea without this detailed business plan and feasibility analysis. A failure to take a strong decision without a business plan might mean a make or break of your entrepreneurial career. To the least, it can save you heaps of stress in-between. Besides, performing this analysis and plotting them in the cash flow chart will produce data for the required investment. It will help you to ascertain the perceived valuation of your new venture. You will be able to figure out how much equity you should be willing to offer against the investment amount you are looking for.

This will be your roadmap to create confidence in you by parties willing to invest or lend money in your business. Smart investors will look for your business plan and different financial figures before even considering to invest in your business. Developing a proper budget, business plan, ROI calculation, and cash flow analysis will give you the right position to ask for investment. You will be able to answer different pin-pointed questions including why they should invest in your business. This confidence will show on your body language and in turn build faith in your potential investor or lender.

Relevant quote:

Joel Osteen (American televangelist and author of 7 'New York Times Best Seller list' books): "If you want to reap financial blessings, you have to sow financially".

20. Generate clear idea on how to fill in the gaps of 'road to success'

At this point, you should be done with the vital home works like a business plan, budgeting, and cash flow analysis. In such a case, you should now be clear on the amount of money you are looking forward to making within the next 3 to 5 years, and how much resources and effort you have to bring onto the table. You will also know how much revenue you are expecting the business to generate from its operation within this time. Moreover, you should also know how much you have to contribute from your pocket on this journey. If you get the analysis right, you will have a clear picture of the gaps. You should know what you have right now and how much more resources are required to be brought from outside to get the business moving as per your expectations.

Before moving further, let me clarify what I meant by the term 'resource'. At the bottom line of the meaning, I meant 'money'. Anything you do (that includes your time and opportunity cost as well) or buy, and anyone you hire to do your job, you need money to pay for the cause. However, to calculate the amount you require, you first need to ascertain the proper 'heads' of resources. For example, you are brainstorming on the required number of office staff to achieve the growth you planned. Apart from direct costs like salary, you also have to remember that with every new staff you will require a set of tools to ensure productivity. These tools include computer, chair, desk, furniture and stationeries to bring in that positive result you are expecting from him or her. You have to consider your salary in the resource analysis as well.

So, now that we are clear on the term 'resources', let's move ahead with our previous discussion. At such a beginning stage of the business, it is very hard to identify exactly how you will mitigate the 'gaps' in your journey. Still, an overall plan is needed on how you want to close the gap. It can be through taking Angel Investment from friends-family-fools (!), or you can consider bank financing if you can offer proper collateral. If you have already developed the MVP and are generating some revenue, then you can also consider VC (Venture Capital) funding. Whatever the way is, you have to have all the options open and explore all the ways simultaneously.

Relevant quote:

Bill Cosby (American former stand-up comedian, actor, musician, and author): "To succeed, your desire for success should be greater than your fear of failure."

21. Take good business partner(s)

This is a very critical issue that quite often turns out to be a 'make or break' matter of a startup, and to some extent a person's entrepreneurial journey. You might have the best idea in the world, can be the best coder or business development person, or the best strategist in your bracket; but one thing is for sure, you cannot do everything by yourself. A business has many factors on the way to its success. On one side it's the technical capabilities and operational know-how that will help you make a good product or value proposition. Whereas, on the other side, a greatly designed product or service is less likely to flourish without good marketing, sales, and service drive. Even so, someone will need to take care of the overall office administration including HR, Accounts, and finances. It is highly unlikely that a single person has all the capabilities and can manage all that stuff alone. This is why you need to have trusted resource(s) who you can depend on with critical responsibilities.

You always have the option to hire befitting resources to carry out those tasks. Nonetheless, the fact of the matter is, most probably you have a very limited resource at this stage. You need to use them very wisely until you get fresh funding either from business revenue or external sources. So, spending your limited money on high-cost resources most probably is not the recommended idea (unless you have a very deep pocket).

Taking into account that you cannot hire the best resources in this cash crunch stage of your startup, it is best to look for a trustworthy and value-adding partner(s). You can share these critical responsibilities with them and run the business as aptly as possible. An employee is less likely to share the same spirit of an owner at a 'low return' environment as well. Now the next million-dollar question comes; how to select that good partner? You will find a lot of people who would want to become partners on a trivial response. However, when you give a good and deep thought, you will find a good partner a very hard to find species!

The prime mover in choosing the right partner should be his or her ability to close the gap to your road to success. He or she should be able to become the critical resource to deliver the required result with passion and commitment. Say, in case you are developing an IT product, and you are the primary engineer to develop the software. You might want to look for a person who is good in the business sense. Your partner should help you to develop and execute proper business development strategies while you develop the product or vice versa. Similarly, a partner might come in with only cash investment which is also a critical resource. The main point is to have complementing partners who together will form a balanced team. Hence, you have to first identify what sort of partner(s) you need to form that ideally balanced team. Also please keep in mind that your best friend should not necessarily turn out to be the partner you are looking for!

In a nutshell, the focus comes to choosing the right partner with the right technical and mental attributes. Even if a person has the right technical abilities, you have to first ascertain his or her trustworthiness and motivation to contribute to the business. I would watch out for the following attributes with almost similar importance:

    a. Ability to contribute to the business
    b. Trustworthiness (e.g. honesty and integrity)
    c. Commitment and motivation to contribute in short, mid, and long term

I have already mentioned the importance of point A. As of point B, you don't want anyone as a partner whom you cannot trust with monetary affairs or you think will compromise your business secret to other parties against other values. That's why, I would like to extend my importance to point C here, which is quite often not considered with due diligence while taking a partner on-board. Even apparently an honest and capable person can turn your business upside down just with his or her lack of commitment and inconsistent contribution to the business.

In my opinion, you should never consider having a working partner who has a full-time salaried job elsewhere. It would be feasible only if the person is contributing financially or purely from a strategic perspective. A job holder will always prioritize his or her job over the startup. Thus, when a contradicting priority arises, he or she is more likely to show the back and put the whole team in trouble in the process. 'Capability to see the big picture' is also a very crucial factor that I would like to add to point C. If available, this virtue helps an entrepreneur to pass through the bad times and tackle any unplanned lean period with patience.

In my case, I have my fair share of a bad experience with partners. I had to deal with overestimated capacity issues where the partner failed to contribute to the business as expected. I had to push out a partner for financial misappropriation as well. I also had to face the (type C) partners where they started nagging about how much they could make if they were doing a job elsewhere.

The type C partner(s) just do not share the same level of spirit like the entrepreneur and it ultimately becomes a burden on both the parties. They seem more concerned with what they are losing now, compared to the excitement of building something that can give much higher returns in the future. These are the people you just do not want in your team as they dampen the spirit in the room and fail to deliver what is expected of them as well. The problem with these people is that they are initially more than motivated to become a partner. There is no doubt they also want to get rich and successful like everyone else by 'doing business'.

Sadly, they completely fail to see what is coming ahead and how much pressure they can handle. Once they are exposed to it, their initial enthusiasm does not take much time to vaporize. Suddenly they feel what a mistake they have made and start looking back to the 'golden job days' when they used to have financial security of the monthly salary. This feeling induces them to start looking for ways to slip from their duties. They start complaining and show an extreme lack of energy in their daily tasks. At best, they can maintain their enthusiasm until they find something better to do (e.g. get into a salaried job). They do not take much to shift to other boats, leaving you alone to manage a sinking ship.

As I said, the type C partners are a 'killer' for a startup and they snap very quickly when the difficult time comes. In my case, in the second year of entrepreneurship, we included a technical person as a partner to become the new CTO of the startup. The first CTO, as well as a partner, got ousted for performance and ethical degradation issues.

The new partner would contribute in the form of 'sweat capital'; means he would contribute his salary as the payment for his common shares in the company. At this phase, I was managing the business operations while meeting family expenses from part-time job income. In a few months, his initial enthusiasm faded away and he started nagging about how hard his life has become without any fixed income. He would daily nag about how much he could earn if he was doing a job. Even though he had scopes to do personal projects to get cash like me, he did not seem very keen on them. After a few months, suddenly he stopped coming to office calling a sick leave. After around two months of remaining absent in the office, he e-mailed his resignation mentioning of critical heart illness. Within a month or two, we heard that he has joined another software firm as a senior programmer. Even though he had lost his moral standing on the business, later we had to buy out his share just to get him out of the team. So getting rid of a non-responsive and/or vicious partner also costs you money!

So, how do you reckon a potential partner's commitment before actually taking him or her into business? My suggestion would be to ask for a small contribution before joining the team. The contribution can be in the form of developing a strategy or a small project work. However, in my opinion, the best way to test a potential partner's energy is to involve him or her in the business plan and budget development process. This is such a painstaking and detail-oriented task that this surely will bring out a potential partner's true reflection of the inner enthusiasm of being engaged in the business (even yours as well). A person with wishful thinking to become the owner of a business at a very low cost will surely turn his or her back when asked for some serious contribution even before joining the team.

Relevant quote:

Michael Eisner (American businessman, Ex-Chairman and Ex-Chief Executive Officer of The Walt Disney Company): "It is rare to find a selfless business partner. If you are lucky it happens once in a lifetime."

Seed phase

22. Hire based on potential, not entirely on skill

Who does not want to get the best available resources to get the jobs done? We all do. If possible, I would love to hire the best person in the world and achieve the best effectiveness and efficiency from the very start. However, the fact of the matter is, the best available resources are also the highest priced in the market, and this is where your ability might be extremely limited.

When hiring the best resources is too expensive, then hiring the most capable fresh minds are the best options. They are relatively cheaper to hire, quick learners, and deliver as you expect once they are ready. You only need to teach them to do things in your way. Finding those above-average brains in the recruitment process is like finding a needle in the haystack. You certainly will not prefer to have anyone in the team who will come to you with problems only, but no alternative suggestions in hand. To be able to find people with the right mindset and capabilities, you need to filter through the recruitment process.

Let me tell you what I do to filter out the above people in a pure recruitment test setup. First, I take a written exam (especially the junior positions) which includes only job-relevant material. For example, if the position is a sales and marketing job, I put only basic sales and marketing related stuff. However, by 'basic' I don't mean asking them to define so and so. Rather I put different scenarios and see their ability to analyze and understand a situation and come up with the solution based on their novice ideas. I mostly do not see the exact result, rather I see their approach to solve it. It tells a lot about their character and capabilities. During the tests, I take the exam on computers and let them use the internet so that they can access all the available resources. I try to see whether they just copy-paste certain information of a seemingly straight forward task or tailor the information before putting them on the answer sheet to match with the exact task.

If suitable, I also take IQ tests to gauge their mental capabilities. In addition to the written test, IQ tests give a great insight into a person's generic internal thought process, and analytical abilities. This method gives me an in-depth idea of candidates' capacity to act independently and problem-solving skills.

The written test is then followed by a face to face interview. I normally look into the visual appearance of the candidate and try to get a feel of his or her general attitude toward life and assess their match for the required role. Just like many other people, I also mainly take refuge in the given CV and try to know more details of the person before the interview.

In the case of technical people, you need to assess their knowledge and skill level. Technical knowledge takes time to learn and get them to learn while on your payroll may be too expensive in the short run. Nonetheless, if you hire a coder with very good basics with an apt to learn quickly; it's highly likely that it will pay off rather quickly.

On the flip side, there are times when you willfully need to pick low capacity people! You can hire them for regular repetitive jobs that have a low scope of innovation and lacks variety. Picking high caliber resources for these roles will be counterproductive as they would rather switch jobs off boredom and lack of learning scope. High potential resources seek jobs with higher variabilities where they can exercise their potential and climb up the ladder.

Relevant quote:

Peter Schutz (Ex-President and CEO of Porsche, motivational speaker, and entrepreneur): "Hire character, train skills."

23. Invest in good HR

An area where a good lot of companies make a huge mistake is that they mix up between hiring good resources at a minimum price and hiring cheap resources. I have already described my way of hiring a good resource based on potential in the previous section. The best part of following this method is that you get to hire people with high potential at their young age at a much lower price. The primary reason being they are yet to develop the required skills (and market primarily pays for skills). Also, take note that paying the resource too low at this stage will put you into the risk of losing him or her within a short time. It won't take much time for that particular resource to get a better offer from another company once he or she develops the minimum required skill set. So, getting a good resource at a low rate does not necessarily mean a cheap hire!

Now let's come to the discussion on what I have meant with 'cheap hire'. Once you float your recruitment circular, you will end up receiving quite a good number of applications for that position. Among them, you will find people with varied skills and potential. People with low potential are not meant to do any cutting-edge and complex tasks and if given such a task, a disaster follows. They are the best fit for repetitive and routine tasks.

The best part of low potential workers come at relatively low cost. You can always hire them; however, you have to set the requirement straight for this position. Even after proper training, you cannot expect them to solve any new challenges unless you explicitly show them how to do it or solve them. It can be expected that most of the candidate pool will come with low potential.

Whereas high potential resources, given the right type of training and job may add great value to your organization. They have the potential to become good leaders. They can perform complex jobs and come up with creative output on the challenges they face within available resources. They are a good fit for product and business development as it demands solutions to challenges with novelty.

Don't just hire cheap resources because they are available, rather hire worthy resources at the lowest possible cost. After all, a cheap and unskilled hire will cost you more due to the flaws, delays and rework in the production process. Based on my experience, the following matrix should give you a good idea on my thoughts about recruiting resources:

	Potential	
Skills	**High Skill, low potential** Good for repetitive jobs, with low to medium aptitude. Moderate price hire. Given right benefit and job security, will become loyal employee.	**High skill, high potential** Best resources, most expensive hire with complex aptitude. A startup generally can't afford such mind in the initial phase, unless having as a partner.
	Low Skill, low potential Good for repetitive jobs, with low aptitude. Very cheap hire. Train to take them to high skilled category ASAP.	**Low skill, high potential** Quick learner, medium to high-medium aptitude, good for future complex jobs. Relatively low cost (but not cheap) hire, potential for great return if loyalty can be attained

Being an entrepreneur, you should carefully analyze the job role and select the right candidate for the position. Selecting the wrong type of person and investing in him or her will, in turn, lead you to financial and time loss.

Relevant quote:

Chinese proverb: "If you pay peanuts, you get monkeys."

24. Develop resources

As the entrepreneur, it's your primary task to figure out which role would you play in the business and the required roles for which you need to hire resources. Once you are sure on the immediate hire requirement, you go for hiring. Depending on the role type, as discussed in the previous sections, you should wisely choose the resources. You can go for a hire or invite someone to become a partner in your new venture.

Bearing in mind the lack of financing capabilities, your next priority would be to hire the right resources for specific roles and train them up ASAP. The sooner you can train them up, the sooner you can delegate them the operational tasks and start focusing on higher priorities.

As discussed in the previous section, your target regarding the low potential resource would be to master them in repetitive jobs. For people with high potential, you need to teach them the basics so that they can get hold of the job and start to develop their roads with your guidance. It's the quality of your invested time and the correctness of your hire that will determine whether you will truly be able to delegate the tasks properly in the end. It will let you engage yourself in more meaningful and value-adding tasks.

Relevant quote:

Steve Jobs (American business magnate, investor, Ex-chairman, chief executive officer, and co-founder of Apple Inc.; Ex-chairman and majority shareholder of Pixar): "Hiring the best is your most important task."

25. Hire fast, fire fast:

A large corporate entity has to follow certain procedures to recruit a resource. To ensure clarity and compliance, they have to take a long road of posting circular in newspapers or online job sites. It follows with wait to get responses, take formal steps for evaluation involving different stakeholders, and finally recruiting. As many departments are usually involved in this process, it generally takes a few weeks or months to complete the process.

On the upside, you as a startup have advantages in this regard. As the decision is very centralized and involves no bureaucracy, the process as a rule of thumb takes very low time. You aren't either bound to publish the recruitment notice publicly. Rather you can search from your channels for good recommendations and get the recruitment process started on a day's notice. Just like the quick start of the process, you can wrap it up quickly too as you have all the authority and decided what sort of person to hire. My fastest time to recruit a person for a business development position is three days (from requirement generation to finalizing a candidate).

Agility is the comparative advantage of a startup, and the entrepreneur should utilize it fully. Corporate job quitting entrepreneurs sometimes get too molded in the bureaucratic process. The sooner they learn to be brisk the better it is for them and their startup.

Even after being rigorous, it is still possible to hire the wrong person. Within a short time after they join your team and you start to engage him or her in work; you get to gauge if the person is a good fit for the role. You will also understand whether he or she is coping well with the position. If you get a negative vibe, then my suggestion would be to directly talk to them and try to get into the root cause of it soon. You should try to comprehend the reason behind their low performance. You should try to rule out any realistic and solvable challenges that he or she may be facing.

Consequently, you might find out that:
(1) The challenge is beyond solving.
(2) You may feel that the person is not motivated enough to

perform well.
(3) You may have misjudged his or her existing skill level which is lower than minimum acceptable standard.
(4) You may figure out that training them would be too expensive.

In the case of (1) and (4), you should directly show the resource the exit door. In the case of (2) and (3), you should give the person a strict timeline to improve the performance. If that does not happen within that timeframe, my suggestion would be to not linger it further and let them go.

Practically the initial misalignment should pop up within the first week or two, and the follow-up activities should not take more than a month (or max two) to complete. Bearing in mind that there has been an agreement on a probation period (Commonly the first three months after joining), this time frame shall suffice to prove their worth. As per the agreement, you can terminate the job on a day's notice (and vice versa).

In reality, most employers feel obligated towards the employees and the wellbeing of the employees' dependents and it hinders them from firing them. Employers also don't recognize the wrong decision they made at the first place by hiring him or her. In such cases, the employer tends to linger the job tenure in the hope that things will improve, which usually do not happen. I also have my due share of such stories where I lingered on with a few resources unduly for months until they got another job and left. I was glad that I didn't have to fire them mid-track and bear the moral burden for any challenge that the employee's family might have to face.

The problem with this 'gracious' approach is that the entrepreneur and the business are strongly hit with this indecisive and benevolent step. It might make you look like a very kind and generous employer but in the process the non-value adding resource eats-up a lot of value off your business itself. The entire time they stay with you, they contribute very less. They halt your advancement and deplete crucial financial resources in the form of salary and other relevant variable expenses. The more they stay, the more you are delayed to get a replacement and train them up to perform up to the mark. On top of that, this also sends out a negative signal within your organization that performance is not a dominant factor to continue the job. In total, bad recruitment might cost you losing six months to even a year worth of salary for the position, which could be easily curtailed.

Thus, right after noting down the initial misalignment, I would strongly suggest you identify the underlying issues and take action(s) within a fixed timeline. This should never exceed a month's timeline. You should firmly monitor changes in their motivation and working approach during the work in progress. Even after all the hard work and set timeline if it does not work out positively; you should have no confusion in showing that particular resource the exit door. If it is within the probation period, then the cutoff should be done on the very day of the final evaluation is completed. As a last alternative measure, you might consider increasing the probation period and confirm his or her position in the team only when you are satisfied. This will surely save you money besides building a performance-based culture in your organization.

Relevant quote:

Unknown: "The longer the process takes, the worse the hire usually turns out."

26. Outsource works to able people

To grow a business, you need to perform 360° responsibilities. On one side, you need to develop your technical platform, and on the other hand, you need to take care of your sales and marketing and deal with customer service. On top of that, you need to check up on regular office maintenance and support services like admin, finance, HR, and others. The fact of the matter is, you cannot be successful by ignoring any aspect. Everything needs to be done effectively and efficiently.

Here comes the challenging part, it is not financially feasible for you to recruit well-skilled people for every sector. Then again there are tasks that you need on an occasional and/or project-basis. There might be just not enough work for a full-time employee. In some cases, recruiting unskilled people and training them up is too expensive. There is simply no room for error in tasks like maintaining the accounts, activating promotional and advertisement campaign or designing the user interface of your software.

Pertaining to your needs, you can strongly consider outsourcing a few tasks to able professional hands. They will make sure to do things first-time-right and deliver you as expected. Mainly you can consider outsourcing the supporting and occasional activities. For example, for a small-scale software product company, outsourcing the graphics user interface design is a one-time job. You don't need to keep a full-time graphic designer for the purpose. You can easily outsource it to an agency or a freelancer. Secondly, you can outsource low complexity, repetitive works; like customer hotline and primary customer complaint handling services. Routine finance and accounts activities can be outsourced as well.

Likewise, some works are best handled by a specialist only (e.g. yearly tax return, legal documentation, etc.). Handling these tasks by yourself (primarily to save money) will kill huge time and become too complex. Keeping busy on every aspect will sum up a high opportunity cost. You would rather do other value-adding tasks with your time and effort.

While you engage in low skilled (with upfront low cost) people in a certain task, you have to accept that errors will take place. The matter of 'first time right' will be a farfetched target for you to achieve. So, doing things in-house might apparently seem like a cheaper option. Anyhow, it will come with a high rate of revisal and your constant monitoring effort. A lot of startups (even large companies) run with the strategy of doing everything in-house. It comes at a higher cost, lower quality and delayed deadlines.

At first sight, outsourcing may appear to be expensive. The higher cost is well justified through delivery on time and a rework proof solid output. Right people with the right skill set and attitude are critical for the growth of a startup.

Relevant quote:

Peter Drucker (Austrian-born American management consultant, educator, and author, whose writings contributed to the philosophical and practical foundations of the modern business corporation): "Do what you do best, and outsource the rest."

27. Create the MVP and hit the market ASAP

Now that you have got everything aligned and all the visible challenges sorted out or well thought out; it is the time for you to push the accelerator. Your first job is to make your product/service offerings good enough to draw in the first revenue, which is also known as the MVP (Minimum Viable Product). As discussed earlier, you need to chalk out the whole MVP plan well ahead. This plan should include the required technical and commercial resources, a clear timeline, and financial cost to achieve it. The cost should not only include the technical resource cost, but also the salary of other staff, your office expenses, and ideally your opportunity cost as well.

Developing the MVP is an extremely critical factor that might become the make or break factor of your startup initiative. An MVP will help you to get critical market feedback about your product. It will help to review your initial assumptions on what you thought to be a good final product. An effectively launched MVP will expose you to the critical drawbacks of your product/s. It will extract the real feedback of the market on the value of your product or service offering.

MVP is an ultimate testbed of your product. The best part of MVP is that you keep your initial investment at a minimum while you get real and effective market feedback. Trust me, the feedback that people will give while paying (or at free pilot phase) for your service will be much more realistic, market-oriented and merciless than getting feedback on the concept note. No matter how good things look on PowerPoint or MS Excel, the product performance on the ground is the first major moment of truth. The perceived vs real value delivery (of your product or service) will give you a good direction on the marketability of your product. At least it will show you the way forward and what to develop to make it a truly viable product.

However, it is really important to have the MVP as an MVP only. Many a time, an entrepreneur gets into an illusion of creating the best product in the market at the first shot and delays too much to bring out the MVP. In the process, they destroy critical resources. I'll discuss this matter more elaborately in the next section.

Relevant quote:

Reid Hoffman (American internet entrepreneur, the co-founder and ex-executive chairman of LinkedIn, venture capitalist and author): "If you are not embarrassed by the first version of your product, you've launched too late."

28. Perfection costs too much; improve as you grow

Given the option of choosing between a perfect and an imperfect product with glitches, what would you choose? Certainly, the first one. Everyone wants perfection and being an entrepreneur, you better be perfect when you deliver your product.

However, no matter how ideal it sounds, perfection has a big cost attached to it. In my opinion, the amount you spent on developing an MVP; you will need to spend 100 to 1000 times more to create a perfect product that is rightly designed for your market. Even then, I am not sure if the required 'perfection' will be achieved. As you develop a perfect product and offer the perfect service at the perfect price; within a short time, the market will respond with a renewed expectation. Thus 'perfection' will have a new target to achieve. So, trying to come up with a perfect product is not only an imperfect thought, it is rather an impossible task in the long run. The cost linked with R&D and business intelligence will be too high to develop at a go.

For example, Microsoft commercially launched Windows 1.0 in 1985, and then Windows 2.0 and 3.0 in 1987 and 1990 respectively. The latest version of Windows (10.0) was released in late 2015. Each version has been modified according to market feedback and has been more bug-free and equipped with richer features than the previous version. We can conclude with confidence that that newer versions of Windows will come out in the future as well. So, even a mega organization like Microsoft is still searching for the 'perfect' product. We won't need to move till W10.0; even if Microsoft would try to jump to W3.0 at the first go, most probably Mac would still be running the show. Microsoft would be bankrupt way before 1990 as it would have spent too much on market research and would not be able to meet that expense without any moving revenue.

Rather, the smartest move is to create a basic platform by developing the MVP with the minimum features and then developing the next level features on top of them. As discussed earlier, it is the most cost-efficient method of developing a product as it engages the minimum resources. It is based on a customer's real market-based requirements, not based on your assumptions.

Above all, product development is a very costly matter and needs to be sustainable. The cost of tech and commercial teams along with the office running cost is pretty high for a startup. Unless you have a deep pocket investment, it won't be possible to keep on developing. Even in case you receive an investment, you need to show your investor(s) the required traction and positive market feedback. So, anyway, you need to develop an MVP and move with it first.

That's how the developed product version releases followed by an MVP will be a most likely match to other similar customers and will require minimum customization while scaling up. In this method, you get to develop exactly as per the market requirement with a fail-proof product development strategy.

Relevant quote:

Sheryl Sandberg (American technology executive, the chief operating officer of Facebook, activist, author, billionaire, and founder of Leanin.org): "Done is better than perfect."

29. Focus more on effectiveness than on efficiency

We all know the proverb, 'smart work beats hard work', which invariably points out the importance of efficiency in the value delivery process. However, keeping the point in mind, you must also remember that efficiency does not count without effectiveness.

If you look at all the inventions, all of them delivered their core values first and then they were built more efficiently over time. Say, for example, a basic google search has revealed, the first stationary gasoline engine car that was patented by Mr. Carl Benz was a one-cylinder two-stroke unit. It ran for the first time on New Year's Eve in 1879. It had a 1.5 horsepower engine allowing the vehicle to reach a maximum speed of 16 km/h. on average. Whereas, roughly 140 years later, supercars like Hennessey Venom F5 (model 2018) has a whopping 1600 horsepower engine with a maximum speed of 301 km/h! The concept of 'car' has remained the same, but the efficiency and output have changed significantly. However, maybe none of that would be possible if that 1879 model did not start its journey properly.

If you already have not secured a good amount of seed funding by now, most probably you are spending from your bootstrapping funds to develop the MVP. This means, you are under tremendous pressure to manage your business. At this moment, you feel the urge to hire the best available resources, because you need to make the money machine running ASAP. However, your fund simply does not allow you to do that. So, you finally end up with the B, C, or even D category people and train them up to deliver as soon as possible, which will again incur cost and take time.

Your product development timeline will receive major bumps in the form of developer problems, server crashes, sudden employee turnover, cash shortages, and many other things. Even then, the final output of your MVP will be something like a cake that is hand made by you for the first time. It simply will not be possible to look at it and feel satisfied!

The success of being an entrepreneur lies in not getting your spirit dampened by those shortfalls. You must keep on pushing as long as there is a chance. May be your target was to move ahead by a foot, but at the end of the day, you may find that you have moved only an inch. Being an entrepreneur, you can't always ensure efficiency with your limited resources. Your primary focus should be to ensure not being stagnant. You need to move forward, even if that means only a bit.

You can achieve efficiency once you are done with developing your product to a certain extent and people are paying you. Customers pay as it delivers at least a minimum quality. The money can be then plowed back to making the system more efficient so that you can increase your profitability; but before that, you must ensure a running revenue stream.

Relevant quote:

Philip Kotler (American marketing author, consultant, and professor): "When it comes to efficiency and effectiveness, I would always start with effectiveness. I am interested in achieving a certain outcome. Only secondarily do I worry about achieving it as efficiently as possible".

30. Delegate to able resources

In the previous section(s), I have put significant emphasis on hiring the right resources. To you as an entrepreneur, the right resource may not necessarily be the most skilled one. Rather, he or she should be the most capable one who will learn quickly to provide critical support when the time comes.

Depending on how quickly you develop these resources, you need to get them ready to take over your operational tasks. It will let you concentrate on more value-adding and strategic activities like business development, raising investment, preparing break-through presentations and proposals, and so on. Your success will depend upon your ability to create suitably competent resources and delegating tasks to them ASAP. This will give you that vital space in your daily activity that will enable you to create more value; be it on generating short term income, or focusing on your long-term missions.

However, before delegating, you need to put the required metrics in place. You have to be able to measure their performance at the end of the day. You have to make sure that nobody can take you for a ride while they enjoy their 'freedom' when you are not around. The task becomes reasonably easier when you can emotionally attach your employees to your business and get them to share your dreams.

Relevant quote:

Eli Broad (American entrepreneur, and philanthropist; the only person to build two Fortune 500 companies in different industries. As of October 2015, the 65th wealthiest person in the world): "The inability to delegate is one of the biggest problems I see with managers at all levels."

31. Get involved in short term cash generation

No matter how big and noble your dream is, at the end of the day you need to generate income to ensure your business' sustainability. The same is applicable to your personal life as well. At the end of each month, you need to pay your bills and take care of your family members. To achieve it you need hard cash in hand.

Entrepreneurship is a tricky matter. Some get very early breaks and start to generate positive cash flow from the very beginning. However, for some, it becomes a tough journey that take years to cover the operating expenses. This is especially true when you get yourself into a business that requires the development of a product. Developing a product, testing it in the market, selling it with profit, and ensuring a positive cash flow into the business is a very difficult and time-consuming job. It requires a great deal of cash investment as well.

No one wants to fail, yet some people have to! According to the Small Business Association (SBA), 30% of new businesses fail during the first two years of being opened, 50% during the first five years and 66% during the first 10. In my opinion, the primary reason an entrepreneur quits is the lack of cash in hand to sustain his or her family expenditures. You can sustain working hard for most of the day and endure the lack of social statuses that you had during your corporate days. However, you cannot endure an empty bottom line with no cash in hand to take care of yourself and your family. You will panic at the view of the quickly depleting bank balance with no immediate income possibility in sight. This is the time that the morale is shattered and entrepreneurs quit.

To minimize the possibility of falling prey to such a situation, you must keep alternative short-term cash generation ideas in hand. You can generate this type of cash from part-time commercial activities. If you are an expert in any field, you can offer that skill for part-time commercial engagement. For instance, if you are good at driving and have your car, you may offer your service at Uber or similar platforms. If you have some technical skill (e.g. engineering, software coding, woodworks, writing a project proposal, or anything that has value to others), you can offer them in the market to earn some quick cash.

First, you offer your service to your immediate circle and get their response to the deliveries. Use them as the reference points to improve and offer your service offerings to a bigger circle, and so on. Social media will significantly help you in marketing your services. This approach will give you a much-needed breathing space to concentrate on your long-term dreams, while you generate just enough cash to maintain your personal and family life.

As for me, I had around 10 years of working experience in the largest mobile telecommunications company in Bangladesh. I have experiences in customer care, corporate client management, and customer experience management. I used this knowledge along with my other skills gathered from my job life to offer training and consultancy to different companies. This random cash generation has proved to be THE lifeline on the question of whether I can continue chasing my entrepreneurial dream or not.

One thing you must bear in mind that the income might not be significant compared to what you used to generate in your previous job. So, don't get too much involved in generating more than enough cash from these engagements. Getting too involved in short term cash generation might cause you to lose your focus from the big picture. Nonetheless, on a positive note, when you look back at the end of the year, you might find that you have covered the minimum family expenses from those small involvements. These small contributions have given you a much-needed time to develop your product.

Relevant quote:

Unknown: "Learn to balance a dream and a job until your dream becomes a job."

32. Do not get engaged in more than two activities

In the previous section, I believe I have duly stretched the importance of getting engaged in short term cash generation to sustain the non-productive period (unyielding phase) of your core business. In addition to that, I would also like to draw your attention to the fact that human capacity is very high. Once it is challenged, it can improve by many folds.

Approaching the more stable phase of your product development stage when you have organized your resources well and delegated your auxiliary works; you will get extra time in hand! At times, you will have time to spare and follow up on your team. Some basic direction shall suffice the follow-up works as a routine task which can be well executed by your team. This is the ideal time to consider nurturing new project(s).

This free time is gold! You can utilize this time or it will get wasted in more entertainment and relaxation! You have cultivated your capacities over the last few years which can be harnessed by keeping the momentum on with engaging in other projects.

Now that you grasped the possibility to get yourself into other tasks/ projects; it is also worth mentioning that when the business will get into the growth phase, it would be hard to manage further expansion if you are handing the operation solely. To manage this workload, I recommend not to take more than two business projects in hand at a time.

If you are already involved in short term cash generation projects (not to be overlooked) you simply will not get enough time to get into a third venture. Once, the core business starts to yield enough returns to include your salary, you can drop your side income source. You can then start investing in other mid to long term projects.

Even if you do get involved in a third project, make sure that you are contributing to it at a strategic level as operational activities demand more time. In such a case, I suggest you be a part of a board of directors/ owners and contribute in critical (e.g. setting company direction etc.) areas only. You have to leave the rest of the activities to other partners. If your partners are ok with that and respect your involvement scope, only then decide to be a part of that business.

Once the people around start to have confidence in you; quite regularly, they will approach with offers requesting your involvement (mostly against company equity). You should follow this exact rule before deciding on whether to get involved in it or not. In the process, you may be ignoring some very prospective projects. However, you have to remember that it's not more precious than risking your own core business and the other ones that you have created so far! The primary focus should be to create a money-making project, and then create and expand your empire following this rule! One at a time… and never more than two at a go!

Relevant quote:

Tim Ferriss (American podcaster, author, entrepreneur and early-stage tech startup investor): "Lack of time is lack of priorities."

33. Minimize fixed cost and overhead

Most of us look forward to working in a nice professional environment. If you are a job quitting entrepreneur, you probably have worked in a nicely maintained office taken care of by proper resources.

It will be natural for you to expect building a nicely decorated office of your own once you become an entrepreneur. You would want your office to have an ambiance where clients and stakeholders can visit. The prerequisites to having a 'nice' office start with an independent office space at a nice area with proper facilities. These may include seating and decoration, air conditioning, arrangement for tea/ coffee, proper support staff, and preferably a separate meeting room for your guests. A welcoming reception area would add to the 'properness' of the office environment. In one sentence, you will like to have a polished atmosphere to create wow to your clients, near and dear ones, your employees, and last but not the least, yourself!

The same applies while recruiting people. You will want to recruit the best available human resource to boost work efficiency. Provided there is extra cash, you will tend to recruit people to upgrade office standards. You want to have that top-notch work force to be able to deliver everything on demand.

Every element costs money to acquire and maintain. As an entrepreneur, just like any good businessman, you should categorize your requirements as 'must-have', 'good to have', and 'nice to have'. As long as you are bootstrapping, always start with the must-haves and stick with it until you start to generate revenue. You can consider 'good to have' only when you have enough money, be it generated from revenue or VC funding. However, you should consider affording the 'nice to haves' only when you are trying to fine-tune your business in a later stage of your entrepreneurial timeline. In my opinion, 'nice to haves' should always come from own sustainable revenue.

You have to identify the 'must-have' factors at the early stage of your venture. A 'must-have' cannot be a nice office, rather a place to sit and be able to work effectively (maybe not even efficiently). A 'must-have' can be a desktop computer, maybe not even a laptop, let alone a printer and scanner (unless you are offering any relevant service). You can achieve these 'must-have' requirements by sitting at your own home, or asking a friend/ relative to let you use a corner space of his or her office at free of cost or minimum rate.

At a certain stage, when you start recruiting people, go with the minimalistic approach by searching for office space at the low-cost locations. Initially, you need to decorate the office with bare minimum facilities (e.g. chair-tables with basic comfort, fans instead of air conditioners, self-service model- no office assistants etc.). It will help you to save valuable financial resources.

Once a person quits a job after spending a mentionable time, generally he or she receives exit packages. These packages come in the form of provident fund, gratuity fund, and if lucky, some retirement packages. If you are in this position, naturally, you will be in a relatively more relaxed mood. This scenario, can easily derail your focus from 'must-haves' and make you spend on 'good to have' and even 'nice to haves' at the very early stage.

Depending on the depth of your pocket, you will tend to go for a nice office at a posh location. You will be tempted to go for your room with a luxurious 'executive chair' that you saw in a furniture store the other day. Extra items like nice glasses and lightings would seem a good idea for that added ambiance factor. Even, you can go for a nice managed co-working office space with all the modern facilities with your single room that might cost you quite some amount of money at the very initial stage.

Let me help you to clarify the concept further, you do not need a 'nice' office to start a business. A good number of successful businesses today started at garages and/or own drawing rooms or bedrooms. The initial business operations were done primarily from home, saving them money on fixed costs of running a business. As a new entrepreneur, your primary focus should be to maximize the effectiveness of your own money. You have to utilize your own pocket money in a very frugal manner until the new cash flow arises either in the form of revenue or investment.

It's very easy for me to visualize the whole scene as I (along with my partners) have made this mistake. Initially, we spent too much on matters which could be put on hold. At first, we took an office at a prestigious location (even though it was a shared one). We started by buying the setup of another running software development firm. Along came a good number of employees (from day one, we had five employees; four software coders and one office assistant). We also recruited more 'good to have' developers when more works were flowing into our portfolio. We even recruited one graphic designer to make our progress 'easier' (which was a 'nice to have' at that moment).

Soon enough, our team went up to 12 members with a fixed salary burden of around USD 5,500 per month. Adding the other fixed costs like office rent, utility bills, etc. the cost skyrocketed to around 6,500 USD per month. The money we were burning were mostly from our bootstrapping fund with a few ongoing projects in hand that was 'expected' to generate money in the future!

When two of those projects faltered (primarily due to project management failure at client end, beyond our control), our cash flow was hit super hard. We were scratching the last drop of our resources to complete those projects and cover up the costs. Just within a matter of a few months, our company almost went bankrupt. The reason? Focusing more on good to have, and not sticking to the must-haves.

What could we do instead? Instead of going for new recruitment for temporary projects, we could outsource the projects to other able companies. In this way, we could minimize our fixed cost and could pay them on a milestone basis. As we had a limited number of projects in hand, our resource working hours were not fully utilized. Whereas for other busy companies, it would not hurt them as dearly as us. They could utilize their resources in other projects while this project's work was not moving at the expected pace.

Relevant quote:

Benjamin Franklin (One of the Founding Fathers of the United

States. Franklin was a leading author, printer, political theorist, politician, freemason, postmaster, scientist, inventor, humorist, civic activist, statesman, and diplomat): "Beware of little expenses. A small leak will sink a great ship."

34. Let go of your ego

People by nature are self-centered and inherently selfish. Just like everyone else, you are also likely to respond to the needs that will matter to you most. As per Maslow's Need Hierarchy model, once you fulfill your physiological needs (like food, water, shelter, etc.), you will head for your safety needs (e.g. security, safety, etc.). Followed by social needs (e.g. friendships, social interaction etc.), esteem needs (prestige, feeling of accomplishments, etc.), and finally self-actualization needs (e.g. trying to achieve the full potential including creative activities).

You might have been the head of this or that in your previous job. While you were on the job, you may have been somewhere high on the ladder and people used to take you into account a lot. Maybe you considered it your right to get noticed and respected at all the relevant platforms you took part in. It is most likely that you were fulfilling your esteem needs. Later you decided to quit your job and start your own business.

Soon after quitting the job, the 'reality bite' will hit after some time. You may have been 'something' in your previous profession. However, as a fresh new entrepreneur, you need to keep in mind that you have nothing but the honor that you have accumulated over the years. The rest, you need to develop from scratch on your own. No matter what you were a month or year back, right now you are nothing! You do not have that corporate backup behind you, and your actual authority does not encompass even a fraction of people as you used to have. The sooner you acknowledge this hard reality, the better.

You have to internally accept the fact that people (at least a good number) will not give you the honor that you thought you 'deserved' and used to have before. People cared for you perhaps just because you had the power to do things that might impact their professional and personal life. It will hurt when that colleague who was always so close to you, might not find you interesting to talk to anymore as you are calling him or her to ask for a 'favor'. You might even find that some are not even answering your phone calls. It's hard to accept!

It's a crucial moment of truth. Respect and recognition from others are a very big matter to many, and this matter alone is enough to shatter a few neo-entrepreneurs' spirit. You have to push through this time with positive self-talk. You have willingly decided to become an entrepreneur and you knew challenges were coming. It is one such challenge you have to face with patience to ride over it to make things right again. In this phase I would suggest you to minimize that 'need for recognition' for the first few years of entrepreneurship. You have to set your mind to rebuild it from scratch! In this phase, you will need to forget about who you used to be. You have to develop the mindset of a fresher, and participate in different relevant forums to get yourself acquainted with relevant people (and also get them to know who you are). It will help you to create your place in the eco-system. You will eventually find a new professional circle and, if successful, you will develop your circle of influence.

You have to be clear about what you can offer to your circle. You will find many established yet younger entrepreneurs who are receptive to your thoughts and directions. You could offer some value from your corporate experience, which they might be lacking. At first, you might feel like a fish out of the water with unknown people around. With time, people will take notice if you talk with proper sense and humility. All you need to do is to forget who you were at your previous corporate positions. You need forget how your ex-colleagues used to look up to you, and what sort of benefits you used to get from your employer!

Once you create your domain, you will find that 'recognition' coming back to you, and now with a bigger force and through a bigger circle! Before it starts to happen, you need to be patient and focused on making yourself useful (and successful up to a certain extent). Nonetheless, this lean recognition period will be a good time to recognize the people who are close to you and who are just butterflies of the season!

Relevant quote:

Nouman Ali Khan (American Muslim speaker and Arabic instructor): "If someone corrects you, and you feel offended, then you have an ego problem."

35. Ask for help with caution

One of the primary differences between a fresh graduate and a job quitting entrepreneur is the network and experience that he or she has gathered across the job life. If you are in the second category, you should know a good number of people. It certainly will depend on how many years of job life you had and how much you have climbed up the ladder in the hierarchy. Your network may be distributed across different sectors who should already be established in their positions and have some sort of authority (or influence over the authority). Even if you do not have a direct network, it is useful to know whom to contact to give you a lift. If you are a fresh graduate entrepreneur (or still studying), with no previous work experience and known professional circle; it may mean that you do not have that advantage of personally knowing critical people in different value chain. You need to compensate the limitation by identifying and getting to know the people in your target niche if any in your close-knit circle.

Now, getting to know people is one thing and asking for their help is a different game altogether. Getting people's help in your entrepreneurial journey can make a significant difference in your business output. A well-wisher's small telephone call can help you to set up a meeting with that decision-maker in minutes, which otherwise might require months of hard work to reach. Getting to know the right person, having good terms with him or her, and getting the work done is a matter of intricate skill that you need to develop.

However, depending on the type of personality and family/work background, some might find this task quite daunting and out of reach. Nonetheless, you should not expect any help from others in getting your job done (e.g. finding the right person whom should you contact to place your service proposal, etc.) unless you start talking to people. As mentioned in the previous point, you will find many people turning their back to you and ignore your call for help. Nonetheless, despite face-changes from a few of your near and dear ones, you might find some great help from many others as well. Sometimes a person who you never expected to help you out might just do so.

To get to utilize your circle, you need to properly identify their value addition potentials and estimate how much you can expect from them. In parallel with this activity, you also need to be very clear on what sort of help you should be looking for. After targeting the high potential people in your known circle, you should approach in the required professional manner with proper channels.

The other person's response might of course vary depending on the type of approach you will have. Someone might happily accommodate your request to get you in touch with the responsible person. However, the same person might react differently if you ask to 'help' in arranging the whole deal that you are looking to crack! For example, I will be more open and comfortable to help a job seeking person if he or she comes with a specific request of getting to connect with a particular person for a meeting. However, I will consider the same person immature if he comes to me with the request of 'finding a job'. This shows that the other person is relying on you for the outcome. Whereas, in the first scenario, it showed that the person has some sort of confidence in him or herself, what is needed is just an opportunity.

The first approach is more likely to generate a result than the second. I am not likely to have enough time and motivation to seek a job for someone while he or she solely depends on my effort. The otherwise close-to-heart person might even act differently if he or she is directly sitting in the decision-making role to be convinced. It's a double-edged sword. On one side you have an advantage of getting your message through very easily. Yet on the other side, the person might be on alert not to get into any trouble off compliance issues just because he or she knows the 'vendor' (that is YOU) personally!

So, you have to be clear on what you are asking from whom and also get to know their viewpoints before strongly pushing your agenda. You need to follow their direct and indirect response (e.g. body language) as to whether they are comfortable with your approach and ready to help you. My suggestion is to leverage on your circle wisely and within a limit, which means not asking for help too frequently and/or too much at a time. Let them stay inside their comfort zone while helping you. It will help you to return to them for further assistance in future. Otherwise, you will run the risk of losing the respect of the ones who are trying to help you and potentially turn their backs on you as well. Your maturity to handle the matters will play a compelling role here, don't blame them if things go wrong!

Relevant quote:

Sandeep Jauhar (the New York Times bestselling author of two medical memoirs and a contributing opinion writer for the New York Times): "The only mistake you can make is not asking for help."

36. Beware of opportunists inside your close circle

When you start a business, it's very natural that you will start small. With very few partners and vendors, you will try to initiate activating the wheel of your business. In the very early phase, you might have a close interaction with all the activities and know everything in details. As the business progresses, you will have to depend on others to execute critical activities, while you oversee the situation and assess the overall outcomes. It is a very common phase of a growing business.

Anyhow, in this phase you will also need to watch out if resources get leaked out of your system; not by errors but due to corruption! The biggest setback comes from the closest of persons upon whom your trusts were highest. I primarily assess corruption in two parameters: 1. financial corruption, and 2. ethical corruption.

Financial corruption is the most common in businesses. Like any other business, you get double-crossed in your startup by a partner or taken for a ride by that long known professional service provider. At the starting of any business, the primary focus stays on sales and growth; and very little or no focus is given on compliance issues. Very little focus is also put to establish, implement, and monitor rules against conflict of interest. In many a case, the startup loses its very important cash to fraudulent activities.

For instance, the most common form of corruption is, one or a few of your partners may team up and outsource your works at a higher rate than the actual market rate. As a mediator, they fill their pocket(s) in the process. Some are by nature dishonest, and some may get into this mishap to safeguard their investment at the expense of the company. No matter what happens, it shatters the morale into pieces. Once the trust is broken, the whole team takes a hefty time to shake off the disaster, if the company does not dissolve in the first place.

Ethical corruption, also like other cases, impacts the business a lot. It takes place when decisions are made considering personal interest; rather than company interest. For example, your partner pushes his or her favorite candidate for a certain role in the company;

even though there might be better options for this position. Here the company gets affected in the long run as a personal interest-driven culture sets off and cliques are formed within the system. In time, a person driven, not a performance-driven culture is established that can turn out to be disastrous.

To avoid such mishaps, you need to keep a keen eye on the whole business and try to pick up early signs of flaws. Suspicious and non-disclosing behavior from a partner needs to be observed closely. If they try to keep a certain value chain totally under control and invisible to the others, it ought to be made accountable. Aggressive reaction on even minor clarification queries and weak body language are some of the early indicators that something might be going wrong. It might prove to be crucial in catching an opportunist off-guard and before s/he makes a good dent in your business and morale.

Relevant quote:

Unknown: "There's something wrong with you if opportunity controls your loyalty."

37. Trust everyone with due diligence

Don't get too intimidated by the previous point on backstabbing partners. You can all in all avoid ending up with a dubious partner if you do proper background checks along with market reputation analysis. You should also bear in mind my other points about delegating tasks to proper resources to carry out routine and operational tasks. Then you can concentrate on developing the business.

The main point I want to mention here is that, at the end of the day, you cannot afford to be too suspicious about the people around you and start doing everything yourself. On the other hand, I recommend to not blindly depend on someone who might take this as a scope to fill their agenda at the expense of the company. You need to choose a path in between, which is to delegate work with much-needed accountability and caution.

Like I said before, you have to utilize your network, and delegate works to vital people. In the journey of doing business, you need to trust a number of people with certain resources; some with money, and some with sensitive information. However, do not forget to apply your due diligence in doing so. And again, keep your eyes and ears open for information and news circling you.

How do you apply your due diligence? On a random basis, you should go through different value chains and try to get visibility of what's happening in and around the processes. Try to walk through the activities and relevant expenses. You can randomly go through the accounting entries, purchasing process, talk to vendors and service providers, take the news of specific market trends, etc. You need to make a to-do list that will be stored only with you. Keep the others wondering about what you will do next! Surprise inspection and fear factor should work great as one of the deterrents of corruption in your organization.

Relevant quote:

Unknown: "When you fully trust someone without any doubt,

you finally get one of two results: a person for life or a lesson for life."

38. You are the whole value chain of your office

If you are from a corporate background, you should be very familiar with highly structured and segmented roles shared among different departments. Each department has their specific set of duties to be performed by assigned personnel. The sales and marketing department widely spearheads the show, having the manufacturing department closely supporting the production process. In the supporting role there are HR, Finance, IT, Admin, compliance, and other departments to ensure a smooth business operation.

It's an entirely different scene when you are forming a business of your own. Forget those days when you called your IT support if the printer is not working, and the admin guys if the paper is not there. It is true indeed that personnel with assigned roles and duties will in effect improve the accountability for each role. Yet crude but true, you simply don't have enough money in your pocket to make your company so structured right now. Like I said before, every bit of beauty and structure costs money to acquire and maintain.

In your business, at least at the initial stage, you have to perform every department's work. The work starts from Procurement (purchasing laptop, printer, furniture, etc.) to Admin (setup, maintenance, office cleaning). Then there is Finance (pay the vendors and employees on time), HR (recruiting new resources, negotiating, processing salaries, etc.). This continues to the core Sales department functions as well where you visit prospective clients to generate the all-important cash. Moreover, if you are a coder in an IT firm, then you need to play the role of production as well!

You need to be a multi-tasker to become an entrepreneur and be ready to do even menial jobs which otherwise you would not consider doing. You need to be responsible for the end-to-end value chain of your company. You have no one to point the finger at if you fail! Remember, it's your baby and you need to clean him/her up from every possible dirt and remain conscious about the wellbeing. You need to take care of your organization from top to bottom with the same care and make sure that it grows to a big and sustainable body.

Just reckon that you are starting from scratch and it demands a positive mindset. You have to forget about who you were in your past job and let go of your ego. Also, you need to keep your fixed cost to the minimum, and give priority to your primary keys to success!

Relevant quote:

Stephen King (American author of horror, supernatural fiction, suspense, science fiction, and fantasy): "Amateurs sit and wait for inspiration, the rest of us just get up and go to work."

39. Don't be afraid to make mistakes; however, don't repeat the mistakes

The term 'mistake' is a highly glorified word in the current entrepreneurial world. It is so glorified that the entrepreneurial evangelists ask you to make 'early mistakes'. These mistakes will burn you at an early age so that you re-grow from the ashes to start all over again. Nonetheless, no matter how much glorified it sounds, making a mistake is always painful. It eats up your time, energy, and money. Depending on the depth of the mistake, it might create a definite hole in your cash flow, cause a huge loss of opportunity, delay your product development, lose your critical employees, and the list goes on.

Entrepreneurship is about trying new things, going for trial and error, making mistakes, and learning with minimum losses. It's a game of attrition; the one who dares to hold it till the end normally wins. If you are an entrepreneur, you need to be ready to make your way. While you do it, you surely will find hardships on the road, and make mistakes while trying to solve those challenges. Sometimes you might need to take even a new road abandoning the old one. Even then, you do not know whether the new road is the right road or not. You need to explore and find it out yourself, and through this you are risking your critical resources.

No matter what sort of experience you have, when you become an entrepreneur, you are venturing into unknown territory. While you previously risked your employer's money with your decisions, here you are going to risk your own money. You are more nervous to take strong decisions and thus make big mistakes. Mistakes here might drain down your life long savings, and eat up your very crucial time from the most productive part of your career. The thought of making mistakes makes a person nervous and you will not be an exception.

However, you need to take calculated risks and be ready to make mistakes. Like I said in a previous chapter, efficiency will not be a strength of your startup. You have to digest many setbacks where you will lose time and money. Each of the setbacks will be the result of a mistake, either by you, your employees, or someone else in the value chain. The most important part is whether you are learning from the mistakes and making sure that whatever happens, you are moving ahead.

So, if you embark on an entrepreneurial journey, it is inevitable that you will make mistakes. Without making mistakes you cannot move forward, unless you are too lucky. The earlier you make mistakes, the earlier you learn, and the lesser cost it takes to rectify those mistakes. However, making a mistake is one thing and repeating a mistake is a completely different one. If you repeat any mistake, it shows your lack of will power to find the reason(s) behind them and to improve your performance.

Every time you repeat a mistake, you go overboard wasting some extra resource. This (repeated) mistake could be completely avoided and you are paying for it directly from your pocket. It also sends a wrong signal to the team that it's ok to be negligent and careless and anyone can get away by not learning from previous mistakes. It will have a long-term trickle-down effect on the overall performance and working culture of the company if your business survives the 'repeated mistake' journey.

Relevant quote:

Unknown: "Forget it enough to get over it, remember it enough so it doesn't happen again."

40. Be proactive and future-ready

As discussed before, as an entrepreneur you need to take end-to-end care of your own business and in doing so, you need to commit yourself fully to the business. Most of the time an entrepreneur has to run around either for strategic or operational tasks, to manage people, or see-through a newly arrived challenge, it can be anything and everything.

Even saying so, as an entrepreneur, you might sometimes find yourself in a relaxed environment as most of the balls could be on others' courts at a given time. While you enjoy this sudden serenity in life, it is also a great opportunity to be proactive and take steps to build up your business. You should always keep a list of to-dos in your hand and get them to use whenever you get the time.

If you do not find enough work to do during such a relaxed stage, you must reckon that you are missing out on something. You most probably should have more than enough items in your to-do list. Checking-off these items might mean more effectiveness and efficiency to your company at any given time. If such a 'workless' situation beholds at the growth stage of your entrepreneurship and continues, you should question yourself. You have to question whether you possess the right mindset to become and remain as an entrepreneur.

Due to its physical characteristics, a shark has to move all the time to survive. When you take entrepreneurship as your primary career, you also will have to grow habits like a shark. You have to look for value addition in every corner and utilize your time to the fullest. You cannot afford to relax. You cannot afford to be too reactive and face challenges as and when they come. You need to look ahead and anticipate what's coming and try to troubleshoot existing and potential challenges before they turn into problems.

You have to remember that if you take up the 'reactive' or 'don't fix anything until it is broken' management style; you will have to spend much more time and money in crisis management. This approach will create immense pressure on your team. Most importantly, you might lose very critical chances just because you are not ready with the right product/ offer at the right time.

Your startup is the vehicle to reach your dream, and you are the creator of your dream. You should exactly know what the dream looks like, how big it is, and what sort of (and how many) vehicles you need to get there. You should be able to visualize what shape your startup should take to help you to achieve your dream. If you are clear on your concept, you should be able to proactively develop your advancement strategy well. It will help you save time thinking about what to do next!

Relevant quote:

Spanish proverb: "The shrimp that falls asleep is carried by the current."

41. Make sure to keep your commitment

Almost every business follows a trend. At first, they start by working on smaller projects and delivering small. Once they create happy customers, they get customers' recommendations and become more confident to deliver bigger projects, bigger commitments. You and your startup will most likely follow the same trend.

For initial works, you mostly depend on your contacts at a close circle or their references. They trust in your business almost blindly to deliver their requirements. However, all they know is you, it's you who they trust. In other words, personal trust in you is all you have at the starting of your business.

Remember, you are nothing compared to what you used to be. All you have is your 'face-value' and trustworthiness to make people remember the old you and get you back on track of success. Keeping commitment is the most important part of your business, that's what will make your customers consider repurchase from you.

Why repurchase is important? Repeat customers spend 67% more on any brand comparing with a first-time customer [3]. Let me explain, put yourself in the shoes of a customer. When you go to any grocery store and someone approaches you with a new brand; what should be your initial reaction? You should be skeptic about its performance. Even if you are positive enough to give it a try, you do not spend the whole budget amount (that you kept to purchase that product) for that brand. Rather you take a test sample and purchase the regular brand that you generally use to consume.

However, once you are satisfied, you are more likely to opt for the new brand. Then, you will spend more of your budget on this product instead of the previous buys.

More importantly, there is a trickledown effect! You start using other products of that brand when you are happy with one product. You as a happy client will recommend it to your close circles (e.g. friends, colleagues etc.). This is the most effective form of marketing; as 73% of people trust recommendations from friends and family, comparing with only 19% of people trust in direct marketing from that brand.[4] Which is why it is said that a satisfied customer is the most valuable advertisement for a brand. It incurs zero expense when they recommend you and holds maximum credibility in the market to your potential customers. Also, studies show that the customers who come from recommendation are often happy, and tend to complain less than regular customers.

Soon enough, what you used to be in your previous job, or what a big shot your father is will become a secondary matter, and your new identity as an entrepreneur will settle-in. People will start judging you, your capabilities, and commitments through your entrepreneurial deeds. You have to make sure that your customers find you committed enough to deliver on or before the deadline with the expected level of quality. If needed, you have to be mentally ready to even incur losses to make sure your commitment is kept alive.

Relevant quote:

Les Brown (American motivational speaker, author, radio DJ, former television host, and former politician): "I don't think that as a participant in life you cannot be committed. You either committed to mediocrity or you committed to greatness."

42. Legal documentation is boring but very critical for growth

You will most likely try to check the product-market fit at the start of your business. Once you are confident about it, you will consider moving ahead with your venture. Many entrepreneurs, quite logically try to reduce hassle and increase working speed, by moving forward without formalizing the business. The formalization process includes core legal documents like trade license and other relevant legal issues which consist of legal registrations, tax return submissions etc. However, once the ball starts rolling, the entrepreneurs tend to put this matter aside and focus on more operational priorities that demand time, money and energy. On the way, these legal documents are sometimes ignored completely until it starts hurting.

As things start to work, this lack in compliance causes a lot of friction. At some point it becomes a critical bottleneck to growth even with a risk of complete shutdown. You need to incur some cost to keep everything up to date. It might help you to grab any current opportunity to ensure growth. For instance, to promptly get the large order from the XYZ company, you will be required to submit full legal documentation including tax papers today for the needed enlistment as a supplier.

Also, if your tax papers are not updated, you might get into trouble with relevant government agencies. It might turn out to be a complete showstopper for your business. All the last few years' hard works might suddenly go in vain with the intervention from the authority. They might just seal your office or burden you with an enormous amount of money as tax and relevant penalties.

The legal work process is to some extent cumbersome in most cases. You will find it even disturbing and time-consuming to stay updated on limited resources. However, you will gain a strong foothold in your country's legal map, once you make yourself and your organization fully compliant (and keep maintaining it). You will have strong confidence and be able to keep your head high whenever you face any difficulty and ask for assistance from relevant authorities without any hesitation.

Relevant quote:

Damian Conway (computer scientist, a member of the Perl community and the author of several books): "Documentation is a love letter that you write to your future self."

43. Maintain your business accounts from the very beginning

In alignment with points from the last segment, just like legal matters, maintaining company expenses and income accounts are not taken seriously. Firstly, these accounts are maintained in an excel sheet or plain paper books. However, when the complexity and frequency of transactions increase, you tend to start missing out on the details. Soon enough, the company accounts become hazy and start losing accountability to your partners, and even yourself.

Company accounts are such a vital matter that you will need to submit it to different authorities quite frequently. Whether you want to apply for loans, submit tax returns, apply for government grants, or approach a potential investor; virtually in every turn, you will need to submit your financial information. Without maintaining a proper account, you and your business will simply lose accountability to others. In such a case, you won't be able to even approach any formal lending institution, let alone potential investors. Your accounts statement will be the proof of your verbal statement to others, without it, you have done nothing so far! As a business owner, you will also need to analyze your financial data from different perspectives to understand its trends and pinpoint different scopes and weaknesses.

This tedious work means going through your accounts to calculate profit/loss with pen and paper and spending hours before coming up with a result. Manually maintaining the account will no doubt reduce your capability to analyze the data as per your likings. Each of the sets of information will require marked time to calculate and bring out a result. I would recommend keeping track of the accounts in a structured manner from the very start. There are free online accounting platforms (I use www.waveapps.com) where you can easily keep track of your accounts in digital format. Also, you can operate them without the need to understand accounting principles in-depth and get results as per your requirement just with a few clicks within minutes. You will be astonished by how this practice benefits you in the future. Getting this information from a single click will save you from huge hassle and give you the flexibility of approaching someone of high importance with the latest data at the least possible time.

Relevant quote:

Warren Buffett (American business magnate, investor, speaker and philanthropist): "Accounting is the language of Business."

44. Plan well ahead to maintain a positive cash flow

The reason to start a business and one's goals with it may vary from person to person. A common matter for all the ventures- be it a profit-generating organization or a not-for-profit one is, you need money to run it! Even if your organization is a social business in nature and you are primarily running on a not-for-profit motive, yet you need to pay salaries to your employees every month. You also need to meet all the fixed costs like rents, utilities, and others regularly. You have to have the minimum amount of cash in hand to meet all those needs.

Nothing is worse for morale than a bill to pay without any cash in hand. The employees' morale is also shattered if the salary is not paid on time. Successful business is about maintaining positive cash flow, even more than earning a profit! This sounds a bit weird, right? How can positive cash flow become even more important than profit? How can I generate positive cash flow if I don't have a profit in the first place? The answer is, earning an accounting profit does not always mean a positive cash flow. Vice versa, having a positive cash flow does not necessarily result from profit.

Let me explain a bit, in accounting principle, the revenue is recorded as soon as the sales are made. You can record a profit in that transaction by deducting the expenses from it. However, making a sale does not mean anything unless you can bring the money into your bank account. This is where things go wrong. Many of your clients will not pay you on time, or even after taking your service, some might not pay you at all (turning into bad debts). This means, even though you have them recorded in your accounting journal, your cash flow statement will show zero or delayed impact on your bottom-line.

Sometimes we become so obsessed with generating sales that we lose focus on actually getting the cash into our accounts. That's why some companies might go bankrupt even after showing huge profits in their accounting statements. At the end of the day, it matters how much cash you have to meet your expenses on time, give bonuses to employees, and pay dividends to your shareholders. With that target in mind, some businesses even sell off their products at huge discounts to clear off their stock to generate enough cash. Some organizations even go for 'factoring' their receivables to other organizations at a discount to generate cash on time.

When you fall into such a cash crunch situation where you can't pay your bills and salaries on time; you have no other option but to halt all other priorities. In this scenario you put all your efforts into collecting dues, taking loans from personal accounts and financial institutions, and go for raising investment. The difference in doing these activities during a crisis period is that you have very limited options but to agree with the other parties' terms and conditions. It might mean taking loans at a higher interest rate or selling equity to investors at a cheaper valuation.

To avoid falling into such a situation, you have to have at least a quarter's plan to save your time in firefighting for cash. For that, you need to plan well ahead to manage proper cash balance at any given time. A smartly drawn cash flow statement will come in very handy in this regard. In this cash flow statement, you can put in all your future cash flows month by month (against your known expenses). It will help you to understand which month you might run short in cash and take proactive action to avoid this situation.

To make the statement more realistic, you have to take your previous experience into account. With this knowledge, you can create necessary provision for accounts receivable (i.e. delayed payment) and bad debt (i.e. client does not pay after taking your service) and reflect those factors in your cash flow statement. If your cash flow statement looks healthy even after adjusting all these factors, you can feel relaxed that you are on the safe side.

Relevant quote:

Richard Branson (English business magnate, investor, author, and philanthropist): "Never take your eyes off the cash flow because it's the lifeblood of business."

45. Don't fall in love with your product

Entrepreneurship is all about sustaining failures and pushing your limits until you achieve success. Your vehicle to your success is your product or service. You have to develop the MVP of the product at the minimum possible time and cost to get real market feedback. From MVP, you have to build the product based on pure customer feedback. In the process, you have to have full commitment and dedication to your product. You have to ensure that you deliver your best at each stage of the product development and client handling process.

As an entrepreneur, you might have already sacrificed a lot for your product and truly believe that this is the answer to your dream of success. However, there might be matters that are beyond your control to reduce that dream to oblivion. The product might be too ahead of the market and hence fail to create proper interest among your potential clientele. Your investors might be too skeptic of it being successful. It would be a real ill fortune if you were to be in a country with a yet to rise entrepreneurial eco-system with hardly any investors interested to plow.

In such instances, you might have to take some really strong and hard decision to kill the product. Clinging on to it and waiting for things to turn around might just break you financially by large. You have to keep your head cool, judge the situation, and decide on the way forward wisely. Falling in absolute love with the product and driving yourself emotionally without addressing the reality will put you fast in quicksand.

What should you do? Your product needs to yield the minimum desired result in the market. You have a few options at hand. 1) Halting investment abruptly and scavenging away with anything you get from it. 2) You may consider selling it off at a throw-away price (if anyone is there to offer any price for it). 3) You could just walk away from it accepting your loss.

If you opt to stop investing in it abruptly in the face of scarcity, but feel it has potential with a market which is still not ready for it, deep freeze it for a later time. In the meantime, if you still have some capacity left, start materializing the second-best idea in your portfolio.

I took the first approach with our seemingly unicorn product 'Madviser.' It was a mobile app with a machine learning capability designed to reduce mobile voice and data bill significantly. Even though it won Seedstars World Bangladesh round in 2015 and showed great results in the MVP stage, it failed to get investor funding.

To achieve a minimum number of downloads into people's mobile and to develop a better product, we needed around a million dollars in investment. In the USA and other developed economies, it is an irony that much simpler ideas get to raise a few millions of dollars each without much of a hassle. However, in Bangladesh, it was a different scenario altogether. At the early stage of the startup eco-system, we had access to very few potential local investors. International (especially US and European) investors were not eager to invest in a company from Bangladesh that is yet to put a 'success' mark on the worldwide startup map. We found a similar mentality in Switzerland while talking to many international investors in the Seedstars World Summit in 2016.

At a point, it was evident that the product will become obsolete and we lacked the fuel to market it to a larger scale. That's when my company's contemporary CEO (who was also a partner) jumped off the boat. He moved on to create a fresh start-up bearing another of his idea with a different investing partner. In the turn of events, I was the second person of the company (playing the role of COO), who got to take over as the CEO of the fast-sinking ship. I promptly decided to stop investing in our non-growing unicorn product that had the potential to make us millionaires in a short time. I scavenged everything I had in my sight to start developing the MVP of a comparatively market ready (but less potential ROI) idea for a product named 'Selliscope', a sales force management system. So, in short, investing in an innovative product that was well ahead of the market had hit our backbone hard!

In April 2016, amidst the chaos, disappointment, and panic, I had to remain calm and decide almost single-handedly to mummify our dream-product and move ahead with the second product although it's selling potential was weaker. My company was scraping. I had to take down 'Madviser' from the system as we even could not afford to pay the bills of an extra cloud hosting. Plus, it demanded a person who would provide daily updates into the software system to keep it effective. Desperate times called for desperate measures!

It took me around a year to finally develop an effective MVP of Selliscope in mid-2017. I got customers' feedback and developed the next versions with paying customers! I started to look forward to becoming self-sustainable soon enough. Clinging on to a dying product brought us (me and my bootstrapping, angel partners) very close to shutting down our venture after a good two years. Yet the last-minute good decision to scrap it and a good amount of luck kept our hopes alive!

Relevant quote:

Elon Musk (Technology entrepreneur, investor, and engineer): "Great companies are built on great products."

46. Know when to drop your product, and move to the next one

In line with my previous point, I would like to extend the importance of knowing when to drop your product. Failure to identify that sweet timing will certainly result in loss of money, energy, and notably time to invest in something new. You need to pinpoint the early signs of product failure and then take action.

I will not stretch on an extensive list of points as there are way too many articles and write-ups available on the internet on early signs of product and startup failure. Each article expresses different viewpoints and I would suggest to go through all the points as different points apply for different scenarios. In my startups' cases (so far, I have co-founded four startups), the following were more or less applicable as early signs of product failure:

a. *Too many internal projects in hand*: Investing on a product is a resource-consuming task and, if you are serious, one product is enough to eat up all your resources. When you notice that you are focusing on more than one product at a time, especially during a crisis, it's an alarm. If it's more than two products you are working on, it's a red alarm! Always keep a keen eye on the item(s) you are investing your time, money and other resources on.

b. *Lack of commitment from top management*: In my first startup 'Utsho', we targeted to deliver regional, rural, and authentic delicacies to the doorsteps of urban consumers. We got initial success and good word of mouth from the customers. However, both me and my partner were still in our jobs (he still is) at the time. As it became hard to juggle both side by side, eventually the startup came to a halt.

c. *No visible cash flow to fund a product*: I've already mentioned how hungry a product becomes in terms of eating up time, money, and energy. It is a red signal if you see that the product depth is very high and you do not have any visible means to bring in more cash flow shortly.

d. *Complete inability to predict future cash flow*: A well-planned roadmap means, as an entrepreneur, you will know how much cash flow you will require to keep your production machine running in future. Reality is, you must start searching for investment at least 6 to 12 months prior to your cash flow requirement. Without proper planning, this visibility will come to you in a much less timeframe. It will vitally reduce the time to react and search for alternative sources if you are already not generating enough cash.

e. *Product monetization is dependent on many other variables*: You must be able to foresee this at the ideation phase. If you face such a situation, you can stop initiating a potentially disastrous project! If you see that your product's monetary success is largely dependent on some other platform's success, or the support of a strategic partner, coupling with too many 'if's and 'but's before the monetization starts; be wary about pursuing that product. A strategic misalignment with your host platform and/or critical supporter(s) might end up in the total crash of your product.

Being able to pick early signs smartly might help you to turn around a wrongly managed strategy and save a product from destruction (and also save the startup). However, if you fail to pick the signs at all, a single failed product might mean the end of your entrepreneurial career draining out your savings. Anyway, you need to be able to recognize a hopelessly sinking ship and abandon it before it's too late.

Even if you fail to see the early 'subtle' signs, you should be able to identify the late signs. These are much more compelling and strong enough signs that you cannot but notice. These late signs might include very low response from critical buyers, not finding enough cash flow source with a quickly depleting bank account. Further signs may include having a few 'semi' and 'half'-cooked product in hand with no sufficient money to spare on a particular product. In-fighting, backbiting, and blame game among the management members are also a vital sign of startup and product failure.

Relevant quote:

Sun Tzu (Chinese general, military strategist, writer and philosopher who lived in the Eastern Zhou period of ancient China):

THE IDEAL QUITTER

"Know your enemy and know yourself and you can fight a hundred battles without disaster."

47. Onboard investors very cautiously

Unless you are directly offering service to your customers while having the office in your living room, you will need to maintain certain resources that will incur a cost. Even if you start very small, whenever you want to scale up, you will need funds to meet the increased expenses. If you do not have enough funds in hand, then an investor will show up.

Investors inject the much-needed oxygen into the business. They come up with funds that help the entrepreneurs to go through the initial lean period enabling them to concentrate on business and product development. It lets the entrepreneur stop worrying about how to meet the next month's company expenses including office rent and employees' salaries. Quite regularly, getting a suitable investment on time might mean a make or break for the startup.

Bearing in mind the benefit of bringing in investment into your business, you must check the motive of the investor. You also have to see whether your investor's values match with yours. You have to remember that you are not taking a loan, rather taking in a partner who may or may not become an active part of your business. Even so, whether an active partner or not, he or she will certainly have some influence over your decision making in the business.

Before accepting the investment, it is crucial to get fully aligned with the interested investor about their expectations. You must clearly understand the role he or she is likely to have in the business, and better to keep them in writing. In the future, it will help to safeguard you from potential conflict of power and misunderstanding with your investor.

It's critical to have matching values with your investor. For example, you are looking to establish a 100% honest and compliant company. However, the investor onboard falls short in those values, and they find it okay to not be compliant and 100% honest with your clients. Certainly, a conflict will start to brew at a point. With the funding authority in hand, he or she will try to influence your decision directly or indirectly; and you just can't ignore his or her demands completely to your dismay.

You also need to strongly align with the investor's plan with your business. Usually, Venture Capitalists are much more professional and mature in their expectations. Primarily, the VCs are more interested in getting a much higher rate of return by selling off the equity rather than hanging on to the business for dividends. In case you onboard an angel investor, there is a good chance that he or she will hang on and expect some healthy dividend from your business.

If not a regular investor in other businesses, his or her expectation might be to start getting the dividend from year one, which will practically be very hard to achieve. So, by having a clear talk on investments from the start, you can gauge how well you align on the expectations. It will help to save yourself from a possible relationship degradation within your close circle. In extreme cases of expectation mismatch, the investor might decide to quit with the remaining fund (putting your business in trouble). He or she may also take legal actions against you considering broken or perceived false promises (putting your goodwill in jeopardy).

Relevant quote:

Robert Kiyosaki (American businessman and author): "It's the investor who is risky, not the investment."

48. It might be a double-edged sword to get funded early

Every startup needs investment to pass certain phases. Broadly, companies start with bootstrapping funds where founding partners invest from their own pockets. Sometimes they take Angel investment where an individual invests in the business. This Angel investment usually comes from a personally known circle and said to come from either of the three Fs (Friends, Family, and Fools)!

However, the most structured and largest amount of investment comes from institutional investors known as Venture Capital (VC) firms. Usually, VC funding comes with a good chunk of money. This is the reason why they are much more educated in financial knowledge and takes much stronger due diligence approach than Angel investors.

Securing an investment by selling off a certain amount of equity gives a much-needed cash flow to continue the product and business development operations. It solves any liquidity pressure at hand for a certain period, usually for around a year or so. It's a great relief for the management members as worrying about how to pay the next month's salary greatly hampers the development thoughts. It also pushes the company to go for short term moves rather than building a strong brand from within. In extreme cases, the company may shut down out of liquidity crisis. Securing an investment helps the company to scale up and reach out to a good level of customers that otherwise would not be possible through slower organic growth.

In this phase, right after receiving the investment, the companies usually increase their team size. They increase the relevant expenses on internal matters along with their marketing efforts to reach out to more customers. All these activities shoot up expenses overnight and the company happily cruises along with a happy cash-rich scenario. The extended marketing efforts also result in good publicity along with a motivated employee base from good benefits and social recognition. With good visibility comes better customer response and a better flow of customer interest and onboarding (be it paid or free customers). Everything looks good with quick growth.

Nonetheless, getting access to huge funds in an early startup phase might do more harm than good. Proper spending of investors' money greatly depends on management maturity and the ability to prioritize the most important things. Lack of it may lead to irrational spending on team growth, with lofty spending on secondary and tertiary priorities. This might lead to growing out of manageable proportion and wastage of resources, depleting valuable VC funds. All this happens without much value addition to the interest of the investors.

On top of that, quite sometimes the co-founders' focus shifts to increasing the valuation of the company through short term growth. This may drift the company away from making decisions that will make it sustainable from within. Sometimes the management members tend to get carried away with huge cash flow in hand. Their spending habits become so huge that the company's revenue flow does not meet the demand even in the intermediate-term. As a result, they tend to seek more and more investment. With the flashy marketing efforts and quick growth, they attract a number of investors. However, when this tendency continues for quite a long time (e.g. a few years) without any proper profitable scenario, the investors start to raise questions. At a point, no new investor gets on board. This is the time when the once flamboyant company chokes out of cash crunch and gets into deep trouble.

Quite often, the co-founders' and other investors' net worth gain becomes more important than business sustainability. Better valuation means more share price resulting in more theoretical money in the form of shareholding value. This tendency pushes the board of directors to go for short term beneficial activities to drive up share price and get a quick exit with a good profit in hand. This bubble continues to get bigger until one day it bursts as no one wants to invest in it anymore.

If you dream to become rich by selling off your shares before the bubble bursts, you must play very smartly. Being the founder, it won't be an easy task to offload your shares as people have invested primarily looking at you. Even if other investors make millions by selling the share of the company that you have built; when you want to sell your portion, you will certainly face big consequences. No one will agree to see getting off board of the very person, whose leadership has brought the company this far. He or she is the one who made them get on board this business. On the other hand, any new investor will not also invest seeing the entrepreneur himself selling off his or her shares. It might be considered a sign of hidden weakness that the entrepreneur himself or herself is looking for an exit route. Also, different countries' laws forbid the co-founders to sell off their shares beyond a certain limit to safeguard the interest of the investors; unless any larger company intends to buy out the whole startup.

Relevant quote:

Unknown: "Maturity is not measured by age. It's an attitude build by experience."

49. Awards are good, but revenue is best

As part of the continuous success, and keeping the momentum and motivation on; you must be in a winning streak. This winning momentum will help you to face the stress and uncertainties of entrepreneurship and keep your and your employees' spirit high. Celebrating small successes with others also convey a confident message to your stakeholders.

Winning random awards work very well in contributing to this motivation and also communicates a positive message to everyone in your value chain about your potential. It also generates the confidence of your potential customers to look for your product and service.

The feeling of winning an award is great and helps you to shout out your achievement to the world. People may not understand your product or how successful you are, but they surely understand the concept of winning an award. Securing an award readily gives you the recognition of becoming 'successful' in your category and puts certain weight on your words, product, and business to others. It feels great when the attitude of people around you change instantly about you upon winning an award. It's very difficult not to get overjoyed with such success.

However, winning awards also have its price. You need to spend quite some time on preparation to develop pitch decks, submitting detailed applications, and pitching in front of the jury boards, whenever required. For this, you need to take yourself off from other business priorities that are directly linked with your productivity and profitability. Winning some awards might add value to your business, however not every award is value-adding. So, it is wise to not apply for any and every award opportunity that comes your way. Some awards are attached with long-term benefits whereas the others are just recognition in a piece of paper and/or crest with no follow-up benefits. Choose the awards that will add value to your business's journey.

It's good to win awards at a regular interval to keep the momentum going. However, focusing too much on winning awards will hamper your business activities. This, in turn, will impact your future cash flow. At the end of the month, you need to pay salaries to your employees and also get to generate a sufficient amount for yourself to pay your personal and family bills. A valueless award will not help in this regard but will drain your time. To meet your expenses, you need to make the business profitable and sustainable. You need to develop the business in such a manner that will generate more than enough cash at a regular interval. Bringing home awards might give you short term recognitions and joy and also can help you in marketing your product. However, in the end, the ultimate recognition lies in making your business sustainably profitable.

In my case, from December 2014 to August 2016, my company won quite a few early awards. National Mobile Applications Award (in B2B category), BRAC Manthan Digital Innovation Award, mBillionth South Asia Award, and also Connecting Startup Bangladesh award are among the most important ones. The Connecting Startup Bangladesh award put us among the top 10 IT startups of Bangladesh identified by the government of Bangladesh itself. We also became champion in the Seedstars world Bangladesh round and took part in the final round in Switzerland. These awards added significant value to my credibility and I, along with my partners, were an instant hit in the social media among our known circle. People considered us to be successful entrepreneurs and young entrepreneurs looked upon us as role models, and some envied us as well!

However, amidst the huge praises and limelight, I became more aware of the pressure these recognitions were building upon me. With far less than perfect products in hand, surely, I was moving to a point of no return where failure was not an option anymore. I had to look confident among people that looked upon me for motivation, whereas inside I became very afraid of managing this huge expectation. I knew that my cash inflow is insufficient compared to the huge cost of product and business development that lies ahead. I was almost having panic attacks. The worst part is that I could not share it with anyone, as no one would believe my words at that point and would discard it by saying, "oh, you are being too modest!"

At that time, I decided to pull my company off from applying in any more awards or recognitions. Instead, I fully dedicated my team to develop a strong product that I can sell at a profit in the market and create a sustainable business out of it. Keeping my flagship product alive, I also discarded all the sub-projects my company had that were consuming resources but not heading anywhere in the short run. I intentionally went off the awards grid, to get rid of the pressure of high expectations and make my company truly sustainable. I kept my head low while other startups joined the bandwagon for becoming famous.

As mentioned earlier, some awards come with intrinsic benefits while the others come in the form of a certificate and/or crest that adds value in the product presentation only. You need to identify those awards that will add strategic benefits to your business and put maximum effort to win them. One such award was the Connecting Startup Bangladesh, which gave us huge leverage. It opened up the scope to get free office space at an important commercial location for 1.5 years (that we could not afford to rent in any way) and government funding. Both these proved to be core sustainability factors for my business.

These supports gave me the critical space to make a successful MVP++ product and hit the market for revenue. It also gave me a window to meet the top officials of the relevant government ministry regularly where we could get our voices heard. It also helped us to get in touch with important people in the eco-system.

So, careful consideration in investing time in strategic awards will add value to your business. However, the primary focus should be to make a good sustainable business to make you a truly successful entrepreneur. You need to take your business to a certain level where the performance of the business and the satisfied customers will shout out much louder than any award!

Relevant quote:

Unknown: "The fastest route to revenue wins."

50. Minimize cost, maximize investment

Before moving on with this topic, I need to clarify what I mean by both the terms 'cost' and 'investment'. To me, 'cost' is something that you incur to maintain and do something without any plan of concrete return. While 'investment' is something that you incur with the target of generating more business and assets. People invest in hope of getting something better in return; whereas incur a cost to consume something for pleasure or basic need or to merely maintain the status quo.

Let me clarify in this phase that I have purely focused on investment for financial and business value addition in this section, not emotional or any other gains. Certainly, you can consider spending for your near and dear ones as investment from emotional and 'staying close' perspective. With due respect its needless to say that the primary objective of this book is not aligned with that notion.

There is a thin line of difference between cost and investment; and many people are not able to differentiate between the two. For example, eating out at a restaurant with your friends and family can be termed as a cost. You consume the food, spend some good time, and feel good. However, from a pure commercial perspective, eating out at the same restaurant with a potential or existing customer with a definite target to develop your business will be termed as an investment. Spending on a good-looking office can be an investment if that matters in maintaining a good image that generates business. However, the same spending will be termed as cost if you decorate your office lavishly just so you feel good and can show-off, without adding to the generation of further asset or business.

The irony of this concept is that this definition is very much dependent on personal explanation. As a spender, you can always bend your thoughts to justify your spending. An apparent cost on office decoration to impress your visiting customers can be easily defined as an investment. Although your own ego-boosting may have been the primary reason behind it. You should keep your spending to a bare minimum on your office if you are not expecting many client visits at your new office. You can always increase your spending on 'good to haves' and 'nice to haves' once you start to generate sustainable revenue.

As an entrepreneur, you have a very limited resource to start with. The perfect investment of this resource should be to increase respective capabilities. You can invest in yourself to get a new professional certification that will add value to your consultancy business. You can invest to improve the skills of your employees. You can take good and justified resources to offer better service to the customers that will increase customer satisfaction and generate good profit. After a certain period of business development, you should consider investing in company certifications that will help you to get more upscale clients with higher profitability.

At the end of the day, it's upon your good judgment on how you segregate between a cost and an investment. Many entrepreneurs fail to mark the gap and end up spending on the wrong places and wonder where the money went and what went wrong!

After around 1-1.5 years of starting my entrepreneurial journey, I was busy saving money and cutting cost at every possible corner. At that time, I had a discussion with one of my ex-colleagues, who also took the exit package with similar monetary benefits like me. Interestingly, he told me that he was passing the best time of his life as he can spend more time with his family. He gets to eat out every week that he could not afford with his limited income before. Incidentally, he also had his ambition to become a successful entrepreneur. Unfortunately for him, he had to get back to a job as he got into a cashless situation, way before I was in with no alternative source of income. Too much pressure eventually lead to his physical ailment out of the stress. In my opinion, the root cause of the ailment and stress was the lack of ability to truly identify and prioritize between cost and investment.

Relevant quote:

Dutch proverb: "Cost goes before the profit."

51. Your own salary is nothing but a number

As an entrepreneur, you can run your company in any form; be it a proprietorship, partnership, or a Limited Liability one. Unless you are running it in proprietorship; you must have other partners or directors who can be engaged in running the business besides you. When both or all of you are engaged in it, it will always be better to fix a salary amount for the time that you are spending for the company.

Quite often, this matter is kept open, to align it 'later'. While one particular member spends more time (or contributes more) than the other(s), this open matter becomes one of the most common sources of partner conflict. One partner asks for a bigger share of profit because he or she has invested 'more' time in it, and contributed 'more' than others. Then the other partner(s) become reluctant to share the profit in that prescription and want to split the profit as per the share/ ownership structure.

The active partner(s) must set a price for their given time as an opportunity cost as well as a salary. This will avoid any heartburn and conflicting situation arising due to hours put in by each member. While the active partner(s) are giving their effort in getting the business established, the others get to do their works and run behind their own priorities. Again, there can be an arrangement for 'sweat capital', which means that the active partner(s) get to own a portion of the company share against their committed time and effort. They actively engage in developing the business while the other partner(s) invest money in it. Whatever the equation is and whatever role you may be playing, the agreement must remain in pen and paper to avoid any unforeseen situation.

If you are the active member playing the key role in steering the company to its success, you must bear in mind that drawing a salary from the investors' money will not be viable in the long run. It won't make sense unless you get to create a positive business and generate sustainable profit so that you can draw your salary from there.

In many cases, as an entrepreneur, you might find yourself in a situation without money to spare for yourself after meeting all the month-end commitments like salary, rent, and other fixed costs. Even if you have money in your account to sustain for the next one or two months, yet your sense of responsibility will make it difficult to draw salary from the stored investors' money (if you are bootstrapping, then your own money) if you do not see any upcoming revenue in view.

In such a case, you will find your salary stacking up in your company's accounts as an accrued item. Be sure that this accrued salary will increase over time and you won't be able to draw your full or partial salary for the next few years to come. In this phase, you may have to depend on the secondary income sources. They can be part-time engagements in various works for income to sustain yourself over this difficult period.

As for me, over the first five years of my entrepreneurship, I could draw only a few months' salaries. The income I had generated from sales revenues and government grants were not sustainable. To be able to meet my company expenses, I had no way but to minimize the company costs by not paying myself from it. I aim to reach up to the self-sustainability level ASAP where my company will bear its full expenses including the CEO's salary.

So, how did I sustain over these years? I got engaged in training and consultancy of different projects with the knowledge I gathered from my previous job(s). This secondary activity has been working as my primary income source up till now.

Relevant quote:

Warren Buffett (American business magnate, investor, speaker and philanthropist): "The more you learn, the more you earn."

Growth Phase

52. Get involved in critical activities, let employees do the rest

You should know what is best for your business as an entrepreneur and founder/ co-founder. At this point, you should be able to segregate between core functions and supporting functions. In the long run, you would need to prioritize your involvement between strategic and operational tasks. As the head of the organization and probably the most important and expensive resource of your company, you and your partner(s) should get involved in the most value-adding tasks.

While you work towards the most value-adding tasks, you just cannot ignore the regular day to day activities that are the lifeblood in keeping the show going. Once you are done with the very basics of setting up your business value chain, you must hire employees to carry out the operational tasks. At this opportune time, you should focus on core issues like product development and business development. Regular administrative tasks (like office maintenance, salary disbursement and banking transactions) can be handed over to the employees. The basic customer management activities (like attending client troubleshooting matters, and maintaining operational contacts etc.) should be phased out from personal to-do list once you can set proper resources.

It will be completely unwise to delegate all the matters to a new resource at once. Rather you should handhold up to a certain extent and allow on-the-job learning for that person. It will help you to gauge his or her load taking capacity and attitude toward work. To delegate these tasks properly, it's pivotal to bring in resources that are competent enough to perform as per the required standard. You must ensure that they have the right attitude to cope with the organizational culture. While recruiting, you should keep the complexity and variability of the roles in mind and get the right person to do the job.

Relevant quote:

Dave Ramsey (American personal finance guru, businessman,

and author of 25+ books): "Delegation requires the willingness to pay for short term failures to gain long term competency."

53. Engage the employees with your vision

An organization is like a living being, you need to nurture it to grow. You need to take care of the business; and the business is nothing without its employees. It will be very hard to grow your business without passionate and dedicated employees. To bring that motivation and passion, you need your employees to engage in your business. Unfortunately, at the onset, you certainly can't afford to give them different benefits, just like a large corporate can do.

You still have some comparative advantage over a large corporate whenever the question of sharing your vision comes. Commonly, at this stage, you have a small team and you know each of the team members well. You have the scope to share your vision with the organization along with how they are contributing to it. You share your dream with them and engage them. You can create a direct link between today's hardships with tomorrow's success. You have to sow the dream in their minds too that they also share the glory of the company's success. They need to believe that the company will grow with everyone on board.

The amusing part of getting engaged with a startup is that it's a high risk-high gain scenario. Employees sometimes take the risk of a volatile job life that may push them into a difficult situation. These hardships may arise in the form of delayed salary dates, no special employee benefit schemes, and many other perks that could be available with a more stable company. Anyhow this risk is compensated many folds if the startup they got into becomes successful. Mostly after the initial crisis period, when a startup finally embarks on the path to success, it achieves a phenomenal growth. With its growth, the employees also grow at a similar pace which is never possible to take place in an established, structured, and stable company.

An entrepreneur's job is to sow the seed of the company's vision into the employees' hearts. The employees need to envision what the company can offer on its way up if they stick with it and contribute with all their hearts. As an entrepreneur, your success will lie in effectively spreading your dreams among your employees and let their blood boil in that spirit just like yours does!

Relevant quote:

Reid Hoffman (American internet entrepreneur, the co-founder and ex-executive chairman of LinkedIn, venture capitalist and author): "No matter how brilliant your mind or strategy, if you're playing a solo game, you'll always lose out to a team."

54. Treat your employees so well that they love you

In addition to sharing your spirit, you need to take another bold step! You need to truly love your employees. To you, your employees should be like your children, and together you are striving for growth; it's not just you. You need to truly feel their pain, become a true well-wisher, and help them to grow. 'Helping to grow' might also mean to recommend him or her for a better job, and a wholehearted career advice.

As I mentioned earlier, you cannot afford to spend a lot on your employees; sometimes you will even fail to give salaries on time. However, if you care for your employees, and show them their way to success, you will send a very strong signal to the rest of your team about your positive intention and your trustworthiness. To them, you need to become that big brother or sister on whom they can depend and come to for any help or advice. You need to become their 'mentor'.

Your focus on your employees will have a spillover impact on your business. For your employees, the loyalty to you will also impact the loyalty to your business. If they love you, there is a very strong possibility that they will love the business as well. In such cases, even your ex-employees will continue to be your brand ambassadors and recommend you and your business whenever any opportunity comes.

Employees loving you will also mean that they will be more aware and understanding about the practical challenges you are facing. They will be more likely to accept any inconvenience in the job without complaining too much.

Relevant quote:

Richard Branson (English business magnate, investor, author and philanthropist. Founder of the Virgin Group, which controls more than 400 companies): "Clients do not come first. Employees come first. If you take care of your employees, they will take care of the clients."

55. Accept that you are a stepping stone for a better future for your employees

The startup is your baby, it's the path to your glory, and your employees are helping to achieve it. Although they may share the same vision with you and be well engaged in your business; you have to admit that they are not the shareholders of your business. They are practically not looking forward to having any pie of the bigger picture that you have in mind except for (a potential) career growth. Thus, they are not likely to sacrifice above a certain extent for you and/or your business.

As mentioned earlier, for certain positions you need to hire low skill high capability people at a relatively low price. You have to bear in mind that the 'low skill' scenario will not sustain over a couple of years. Under your leadership, they will emerge as moderately skilled resources soon enough. They will get a good grasp of you and your clients' value chains along with developing other relevant skills up to a high extent. In that phase, it is normal for them to be aware of their market value as skilled personnel. Unless you proactively adjust their salary to match with the reasonable market offerings, there will always be a lucrative world outside. However, the fact of the matter is, often the 'reasonable' price the market is willing to offer for such ready resource is not within your range. Hence you have to be prepared mentally to let your employees go to other organizations with a better salary and other benefits.

This is a situation you cannot control and ought to make peace with by staying cool-headed. Losing your cool in this stage and trying to emotionally blackmail your employees with comments like, "how can you take such decision after all that I've done for you" will only backfire. It won't help you in retaining your employees. This approach will rather destroy the camaraderie you have built over time. Even if your employee decides to stay, it will impact on their enthusiasm and positive energy to contribute to your goal. This will warn the other employees on what to expect when their turn to move to a better opportunity comes up. It will foster a gloomy cloud in your office environment.

I would suggest, let the exit be easy and friendly. You can instead ask them to help you find a proper replacement for his or her role. Remember, you have recruited highly capable persons in the first place and they have good analytical and decision-making ability as well. In my case, it has overall worked out great and the employees themselves have referred me the best resource based on their job-person fit analysis. In almost all cases, I found their suggestion effective. Most of the new replacements have performed up to the expectations.

I have so far found this approach extremely effective and efficient because of a few factors. Firstly, as I mentioned, the employees know their jobs best and thus referrals coming through them have already passed the initial technical evaluation. In this case, your prime check point would be their cultural fit and other factors only. In my case, the salary has often been negotiated by my existing employee, even before the replacement appeared for the interview. All I needed to do was to trust their evaluation, meet the new one, and finalize the deal!

Secondly, the whole process takes a shorter time compared to the standard recruitment process. You can let pass the cumbersome process of floating the circular, waiting till the deadline, sorting the CVs, calling people for exams/ interviews and so on. It might take weeks, or even months, to complete in this way, but the referral method takes no more than two weeks to complete (if a suitable candidate is found).

Thirdly, the duties handover process is smoother as the new recruit is acquainted with the old employee. It makes the old employee more accommodative towards the new person's relevant challenges faced. They have a cooperative spirit and tend to complain less against each other.

However, this approach works only when the employee is passionately engaged with your organization and loves you as a mentor and well-wisher!

Relevant quote:

THE IDEAL QUITTER

Unknown: "Tough times don't last, tough teams, do!"

56. Cost estimation will overshoot, but revenue target will fail

The devil lies in the details! No matter how much you have planned, it's just not possible to forecast all the small details of the journey of your business. You need to look out for unplanned and unwanted situations that will cost you money or at least stop you from earning expected revenue. These events will result in an almost certain cost overshoot than the budgeted amount. They can extend from that unexpected major machine breakdown or that coder of your software who just fell ill one fine morning resulting in a major timeline failure. It could be your critical supplier who simply lied about your product shipment, resulting in a cancellation of order by your client.

It's a major irony that even the planners know from within that the revenue forecast will not be met. All the flowery forecasts (and even the not-so-flowery ones) will prove fruitless in the end because your MVP might take much more time to develop. That feature upgradation that the customer required 6 months back would still be 'under development' that you thought could be delivered within three months. Some things will just not be under control, and you as an entrepreneur have to live with it and be content with whatever you got. You should continue working for a better day, that's the most important part.

Relevant quote:

Henry Ford (an American captain of industry and a business magnate, the founder of the Ford Motor Company, and the sponsor of the development of the assembly line technique of mass production): "Failure is only the opportunity to begin again, only this time more wisely."

57. Raising capital for your business is not a success, making it profitable is:

In the current 'startup bubble', a strange phenomenon is taking place. Now companies are being applauded for the money they have 'raised' as investment. How much money a company has bagged is seen as an initial yardstick of success. In my opinion, this mentality is directly related to the short-term moneymaking viewpoint. This comes from the venture capitalists along with many entrepreneurs whose target is to make quick bucks. They work towards establishing a company, getting some traction in the market, and then selling it off (in part or full) to the highest bidder. The VCs also take their chances to use the heightened share price to quickly exit the company that they purchased a short time back, making very quick profits.

This thought has created many flamboyant startups that come up with lofty concepts. Interestingly they are being valued highly and have raised millions of dollars even from developed markets. Let me cite the example of the 'YO' app. According to Wikipedia, this abruptly simple app is used to send 'YO' message to others (and YO only, nothing else). It was downloaded 3 million times and over 100 million YOs were sent by the users by 2014. This app was valued at 15 million USD in 2014 and raised around 2.5 million USD as an investment from the market. Where is it now? In February 2018, YO posted a message on 'Medium', asking users to donate to its 'Patreon' account to keep the app alive. This shows the downfall of a once super flamboyant app. Nonetheless, I presume many early investors rode the wave at that time and headed for the exit with a huge profit in hand (with the product heading nowhere).

However, as absurd as it may sound, quite a few of these high valued startups do not even have a clear monetization and profit generation plan. Although having a great number of users in the market, these companies do not know how they will make money and turn them into profit. Thus, these companies are not fit to do long term business and are not sustainable at all. Their game is most likely to end as the investors' money gets dried up and no one wants to invest in it anymore. Yet they are valued at millions or billions of dollars; and these overhyped startups are still raising funding in hundreds of millions of dollars.

You need investment to grow quickly in this dynamic market. Not being able to quickly develop your product and/or grow quickly might mean coming up with a product too late in the market. It might mean that either the market needs have changed, or your competitors have already grabbed the demand before you could even push to grow fast.

To raise investment, you need to sell your startup's equity to interested investors after proper valuation. This valuation method is sometimes manipulated by startups by overstretching its capabilities and showing significant growth in terms of users. This fact is then presented to impress the investors so that they decide to move forward with the funding. Once done, the company's official valuation grows. The previous investors and the founders' equity worth also increase accordingly. Sometimes, entrepreneurs and other VCs take this opportunity to sell off their share of equity and get out of the scene with a super inflated bank account.

Also, in this process, don't get dazzled by the apparent vertical growth of the freshly funded startups. These seemingly successful ventures appear to be successful in terms of getting into the limelight. Almost all these startups who got rich from VC funding are not making any profit in the short run and substantially burning cash to achieve growth. They take a round of VC funding, increase their capabilities (or in other words, spending) to a point, initiate hefty promotional activities, and try to achieve phenomenal growth with it. However, if the revenue from this growth is not sustainable, soon enough they re-evaluate their company. After that, they sell off even more shares at a higher price to generate more cash to meet the expenses. It's a happy go scenario where existing investors are delighted as their net worth of share increases.

This cycle of increasing share price continues until the time when the VCs start asking the real questions about achieving the ROI and its financial performance. The VCs are smart people who know that growing too much out of proportion might become hard to manage for a juvenile organization. The bubble bursts when the company becomes over-dependent on VC funding. In this phase it fails to stay afloat by generating sustainable revenue to meet their super heightened expenditure level. Without being able to draw in more cash from the VCs, this is the time when the startup starts to dry out of cash and eventually heads for a close-down. Over dependency on VC funding reduces the capability and attitude to develop a sustainable business. The recent bubble bursts of WeWork and Uber are also two examples that without proper profit, all companies will head downwards.

If you are planning for some quick bucks by selling off your company, it might be a good idea to apply tricks to increase the company valuation, and thus your share price. However, if you aim to truly run a business to its maturity, get regular dividends out of it, and make it a factor in your retirement plan; this strategy of over dependency in selling off shares might even negatively impact you and your business. Although you will acquire some cash for business growth in this way; in the long run, you are bringing in more and more heads inside your business. Some of them might hamper your business plan and try to unduly impose their thoughts to run the business. This will not only dilute your attention from running your own business but also create internal conflict and disrupt your business from within.

Relevant quote:

Fred Wilson (American businessman, venture capitalist, and blogger): "The fact is that the amount of money the startups raise in their seed and Series A rounds is inversely correlated with success."

58. Create strategic partnership for value generation

As the entrepreneur and head of the organization, you must take the company forward and make it successful. However, moving forward does not follow a fixed equation and varies based on your product and market type. You may have to trial with a different combination of solutions and continue until you find an effective one. You will often find that the ingredient for growth and success are not always in your hand.

First of all, you have to define your growth strategy and single out what sort of support you will require. It can be presumed that as a startup you will lack the capacity to initiate growth; both structurally and financially. Neither will you have the ability to increase your sales and marketing team within a short notice; nor will you have the strategic intent to develop and deliver everything by yourself. To compensate for this challenge, I strongly recommend you to create a strategic partnership with different horizontal and vertical value chain organizations so that you can support each other in mutual growth.

For example, if you are marketing a B2B (business to business) product or service, then you need to have a strong direct sales force to reach the potential clients and follow through. The fact is, you just cannot afford to employ a good number of high-quality salespeople to increase your reach. What should you do? You should tie-up with industry complimentary service/product providers. It shall be a marriage that has the potential to help both you and your value chain partner organization. You can also become the sales agent of other established complementary brands that will help you to earn quick money.

Let me share my case. My company has developed a sales force management software. It's a B2B product and works as an excellent tool to improve the efficiency of any sales organization. It works to improve accountability of the sales force members as well as collects information from the market and report accordingly. It can work as the last mile connectivity for any company using an ERP (Enterprise Resource Planning) solution (as an ERP usually does not cover up to the field level). So, we have tied up with ERP solution providers so that when clients ask for such solutions, they can recommend us. We also have a reciprocal understanding where we recommend the ERP solution provider(s) in case any company wants to have upward integration with our software.

As an add-on service to increase the security of the software, we have tied up with a software security solution provider. This both way integration has made our offering much stronger. It has saved us a lot of resources to develop such backward and forward linking utilities. Above all, we want to concentrate and become a specialist in our field only and do not even want to invest in other solutions. Thus, it's a win-win arrangement where everyone has the potential to earn a share of the revenue generated from other's sales figures.

As I said, you can't do everything alone and that applies for growth and development as well. Take proper value chain partners wherever you feel will add value. There is no problem in sharing some revenue if your partners help you to generate it. Remember, 20% of 100 is double than 100% of 10!

Relevant quote:

Milton Berle (American comedian and actor): "If opportunity doesn't knock, build a door."

59. Keep the focus on the big picture

When you decide to turn into an entrepreneur and start your venture; you must have a clear vision (aka dream) to achieve. That dream should guide you through your tough times. Your vision should be able to keep you on track and nudge you from getting diverted by peripheral and no/low-value adding activities. It should also keep you together when you face failures in different steps.

In entrepreneurship, many things will not work as planned and outcomes will not turn out to be in your favor. If at the starting of the day, you plan to achieve a foot, at the end of the day you might find that you have moved only an inch. You will most likely know the reasons, but quite frequently cannot do much about it due to your limitations. It's extremely frustrating, to say the least.

Nonetheless, you need to be relentlessly positive, optimistic, and hopeful in your journey where you will discard all the negatives by looking at the big picture. You need to ascertain, whether you have moved forward to that vision, even if it is by an inch only. Even if every two steps forward mean stepping one back, it is paramount to focus on your improvement. I mentioned before that efficiency will not be your strength up till a certain time of the startup; but you need to make sure of the effectiveness. You need to make sure that you are improving in some way or other and adding value to yourself in the 'big picture'.

Relevant quote:

Eleanor Roosevelt (American political figure, diplomat and activist): "The future belongs to those who believe in the beauty of their dreams."

60. Concentrate on and celebrate short, mid, and long-term success

In my opinion, for a startup, short term objectives should focus on a period of three months to one year at most. A mid-term objective should focus on one to three years, and more than that should fall into the long-term category. As the company matures, the tenure of short, mid, and long term will also increase depending on which industry you are working in. Mostly, companies engaged in the technology sector have shorter-term objective tenures for the quick-changing nature of the business environment and the emergence of new technologies. You, as an entrepreneur, should have clear objectives for all three terms. These set objectives will help you to ascertain whether you are moving in the right direction or not.

Irrespective of your motive (to sell off your company and get rich quickly, or to hang on to make the business a part of your retirement plan), you must focus on success in your entrepreneurial journey. A very few people get rich by sheer luck; and even if they do, they hardly can retain the wealth in the long run. Getting rich by chance is a difficult aspect for entrepreneurs as nothing comes easy for them. Every successful entrepreneur has their story of difficult times that hardly others later truly understand. Even if you desire to sell your company off to a larger entity entirely for short term benefit; at first you need to make the company successful or at least show a good spark to excite the investors.

In case you are in the business with much longer-term vision, you obviously will be looking forward to making it successful as well as sustainable. However, focusing on long term success does not mean that short term successes do not matter. On the small short-term successes, the base of longer ones will be created. As stated before, entrepreneurship for most is a game of endurance. To endure the pain, you need to keep patience. To have the required patience, you need to have proper motivation. It is the short-term successes that will generate these motivations.

Short term successes of reaching benchmarks like securing an important client account (or ANY client at the beginning phase), winning an award, reaching a certain number of clients, etc. need to be celebrated up to their merit. These celebrations will energize you and your team to achieve the next one. However, you have to be able to visibly connect the dots between short- and long-term successes to bring more objectivity to your team members' actions. Without a clear connection and objectivity, your short-term successes will create immediate buzz without making any significant contribution to the long-term ones.

For example, achieving client accounts is very important for the business. However, if you focus too much on quantity and onboard clients for free only to get ahead in the number game, it will come with consequences. It may create more noise in the market but a tunnel vision to impress the current and potential investors will sidetrack you from your mid and long-term goal. However, if the free client onboarding is part of a strategic move that will vitally impact other success factors to make the company more sustainable from generating future profit, then it's certain that this action has more accountability than a non-strategic one.

Relevant quote:

Mia Hamm (American retired professional soccer player, two-time Olympic gold medalist, and two-time FIFA Women's World Cup champion): "Celebrate what you've accomplished, but raise the bar a little higher each time you succeed."

61. Focus on sustainable revenue:

Extending from my previous point, the primary reason I could not draw my salary from my company so far is the lack of sustainable revenue. There were bits and pieces of revenue from outsourcing projects. We got some critical cash inflow from the government grants as well. However, to the dismay, the revenue from my company's product, 'Sokrio', is still at an early stage.

Sokrio is designed in SaaS (Software as a Service) model where it will generate revenue on a monthly basis. In SaaS model, the clients get to rent in a working space of a certain software and pay as per the number of users only. This saves clients from spending a bulk amount to purchase the whole software. It is widely popular across the developed business world. However, the focal challenge for the service providing company is the finance to develop the platform first and then monetize it. A SaaS platform also does not have much scope to get large cash inflows like standard project-based outsourcing firms. The revenue it generates accumulates slowly with the increase of its user base.

However, the same SaaS platform, upon reaching a critical mass, will boost sustainable and significant revenue. It will be enough to create a breathing space to plan on a longer-term. At a certain stage, it will also become scalable where you get to start spending on strategic matters and initiate worldwide marketing. If you can sustain the low revenue period, the best part of the SaaS model is that it comes with highly stable and sustainable revenue once established. This isn't the usual case for outsourced project-based companies that require ensuring projects in the pipeline to avoid the risk of a sudden drop in cash flow.

The outsourcing based companies also strive to ensure sustainable revenue by getting into AMC (Annual Maintenance Contract) with their clients. Nonetheless, at a certain time, everyone feels the need to establish their own product. Companies want to reduce dependency on client projects by forming own product in the market and attain more profit through a sustainable revenue stream.

Relevant quote:

Andy Rooney (American radio and television writer): "Everyone wants to live on top of the mountain, but all the happiness and growth occurs while you're climbing it."

62. Getting a bit late success is okay

It's a fact that life is not fair to everyone. In entrepreneurship, you will see a few shining stars with early success and limelight. You will see them floating in investors' money and expanding their business exponentially within a few years of initiation. Whereas for the rest, it's a grueling continuous uphill drive and struggle. Not being able to withstand the stress, most of the entrepreneurs will quit after some time. For the rest, it will be further stress and agony until they reach a tipping point where the games change altogether. The fact of the matter is that, no one can tell when the tipping point will arrive and how much more pushing is required to reach up to that point.

Everyone wants quick success. There is no harm in that and practically getting it is even better. However, in my opinion, sometimes it's good for the entrepreneur's learning and maturity to get a bit of late success. It is a fact that people get the most of the learning through mistakes and failures; not successes. Whenever you are succeeding, everything seems right with cheers all around. Things get very different whenever you hit a brick wall that pushes you to think further and expand your limits.

If you, as an entrepreneur, get very quick success; there is always a possibility that you might get over-confident of your capabilities. It might lead you to making mistakes in the future that will cost much higher than it would do at your early stage of activities. On the other hand, going through difficulties at the early stage and a bit late success will help you to identify your critical improvement areas and inefficiencies. It will also help you to know your true supporters and separate the 'friends of good times only'.

I became a full-time entrepreneur in 2014 and we (my partners and I) started our software development firm. Within one and a half year of operations, we secured a few good brands as our clients. We got fairly good recognition from the government as one of our early-stage products (Selliscope, a sales force management system) got the national mobile applications award. We also got an international recognition where we became the Bangladesh chapter champion at Seedstars World startup competition with another of our product,

Madviser. It was a mobile application that helped to reduce mobile telecommunication expenses. Through that, we got to represent our country in the final round in Switzerland. Things were looking very good with recognitions and cheers flying all around.

Under these apparent triumphs, the company was bleeding profusely with high overhead expenses and very low income. Our bootstrapping fund was depleting quickly. Our company was developing multiple products where we effectively did not have enough funding for even a single product. As new entrepreneurs, we did not even have any idea then! We hoped that we would be able to onboard a strong investment. At one point of time, our monthly company expenses (without our salary figures) shot to above USD 6000 per month. That certainly was a fairly large amount for a company with very little, irregular, and non-sustainable income. As a result, even under all the recognitions, we were terrified of what the future holds lest we cannot get the reign of the situation.

Failing to secure any strong regular revenue source, soon enough we reached a severe cash crunch. To keep continuing, we had no option but to become more efficient. At that moment (after around 2 years of operations), I took over the company as the CEO, as the previous CEO walked out to pursue another startup with support from another investor. I instantly reduced the auxiliary resources like graphic designers who didn't have much work and the task could be easily outsourced. I also had to demand more accountability in the output of the coders where gross flaws and pilferages were traced. I had to get rid of the expensive resources who were not proving their value for money. Within three months, from a team of 12, I brought the number of employees to 3. I outsourced every possible item to ensure quality and cost control. I had to get back to square-one to get rid of all the rough edges.

Since then I redesigned my team and worked steadily with a focus on a single product. It took me another 1.5 grueling years to develop revenue-earning MVP. I had to scrap three versions of software architecture and source codes when the teams failed to deliver as expected. Finally, with the fourth version (and team), it worked out closer to my expectations. I have developed and fine-tuned the product with direct customers' feedback.

The struggle of the first 5 years of entrepreneurship has dramatically improved my decision-making capability, efficiency, and made me more mature as an entrepreneur. If we could get access to good funding within the first two years, certainly these learning would not take place. I would turn out to be a visibly flashy 'successful' entrepreneur with investor money. I am very confident to say at this point that I would not be matured enough to handle that money well. Most likely, I would waste a good portion of the investors' money on grandiose matters inefficiently. Right now, if I onboard a new investor, I would spend wisely with a strict focus on effectiveness and efficiency. It would not be the case if I became 'successful' earlier.

That's the reason why I become very skeptical of startups with good investor backup that start with a bang (e.g. good media coverage, flashy offices, a good number of employees etc.). I feel time will tell whether they can sustain in the long run. Most of the startups dry out after the initial loud noise. I believe it's mainly owing to their poor spending habits which are not effective or efficient. They got the money in hand too early in their entrepreneurial career.

Relevant quote:

Mary Anne Evans (Known by her pen name George Eliot, was an English novelist, poet, journalist, translator, and one of the leading writers of the Victorian era): "It is never too late to be what you might have been."

Overall Direction

63. Don't waste resources; it's too scarce for a startup

The startup is your vehicle to your dream. It's a basket full of potential, yet right now not performing in full throttle. You have to ensure the utilization of resources to the maximum. This is the point where you may confuse comparing to one of the previous sections (section 29) where I mentioned about focusing on effectiveness rather than efficiency. The primary reason is that many factors will not be in your control and that optimization in resource usage will not be possible in almost all cases.

However, in other sections, I also mentioned about focusing on the 'must-haves', followed by the 'good to haves', and 'nice to haves'. If you keep a strict eye on this baseline, you should be able to maximize resource utilization in many a case. You also need to keep a close eye on 'leakages' from your internal value chain, which can also become a great source of resource wastage and everything will cost you dearly.

I have urged to recruit the best available and most suitable resources at the minimum possible cost, and train them up ASAP so that you can delegate them the routine tasks. Failure to recruit the right resources will drain out time, money, and energy. In another section, I also urged you to hire fast and fire fast, which emphasizes on getting rid of the non-value adding resources as soon as possible after their (lack of) worth was identified.

When you are in a penny-pinching situation, the worst thing that can happen is inefficiency through leakage in your value chain. This might turn out to be critical at the end and might result in that 'only a few thousand dollars short' situation. Put a strong emphasis on choosing the right people in your team, and training them up ASAP, and equipping them with the right tools. If any investment is required, strongly consider investing as spending a few hundred dollars now might save that few thousand dollars afterward.

My main point of discussion here is that you have to understand what is in your control and what is not. The ones that are beyond control have to be accepted as things that might not go as planned. For other matters, you need to design a close monitoring system so that resources are not left unutilized, underutilized, or even worse, wrongly utilized. Even saying so, you have to acknowledge that things WILL go wrong in your journey, and putting a zero-tolerance on going wrong will only increase the stress of your journey. You should flex your senses and move ahead by solving challenges one at a time.

Relevant quote:

Thomas Love Peacock (English novelist, poet, and official of the East India Company): "The waste of plenty is the resource of scarcity."

64. Have a dream so large that won't let you quit

Entrepreneurship starts with a fantasy and some sort of romance. At the beginning, it passes through some time similar to what is called a 'honeymoon period'. In this phase, you still have some money in your pocket. With that, you are recruiting, loving to share your business card with others, and excitingly describing what your new business is all about to your near and dear ones. Yet very soon the reality settles in where things come out that do not look picture perfect. Your product/service development does not meet expected timeline and quality, customers don't pay you on time, and sometimes do not pay you at all. You find it difficult to pay monthly salaries, your standard of living falls, and you spend most of the day thinking how to pay the next salary to your employees. Quite ironically, the month also tends to end quicker than before!

This ugly side of entrepreneurship comes with hardship, sweat, stress, ridicule (by others), feeling of helplessness, and tears that are just not sharable with anyone. These are the times when entrepreneurs seriously consider quitting, and most of them do. When the entrepreneurs' bottom-line gets a hit and they struggle to pay their regular monthly bills along with maintaining their basic standard of living; these are times when startups shut down and people get back to job swearing never to get into business again!

This is a very tough time, and I believe there is hardly any entrepreneur who has not passed this stage of hardship. In the first five years, I have seriously considered to close down my business at least four times. However, what has stopped me to pull the plug is the not-quitting attitude before seeing it till the end. This attitude is fueled by my dream of creating enough asset base at the time of my retirement for a rich retired life. After my retirement, I wish to travel the world as well as spend in philanthropic activities to my heart's content.

Sometimes dream is the only factor that stands between an entrepreneur and quitting. When all things seem to be going in the wrong direction and nothing is falling in place, then remind yourself of your dream and how good it will be when you achieve it!

THE IDEAL QUITTER

Relevant quote:

Unknown: "If you don't have big dreams and goals, you'll end up working for someone that does."

65. Keep 'exit' options limited:

Entrepreneurship is such a matter where sooner or later you will hit a brick wall. You will question yourself whether trying to be an entrepreneur was a good idea in the first place. This phase in an entrepreneurial life is so predictable, that it's not a matter of 'if', rather a matter of 'when'.

The brick wall might come to you in many forms. You may have a complete blank pocket with months of employee salary pending. Your client may create a huge bad debt. Your trusted partner might illegally siphon out money into his/her account from your company while paying the vendors. You may run out of money while no investor is willing to fund your apparently 'great' MVP, or simply your product is taking too long to get proper traction!

If you are not truly determined about doing your business whole heartedly; I can guarantee that your willpower to move forward will be shattered at some point. Once your morale is down, you would be susceptible to considering options to move away from this mess. You also look for ways to cover the opportunity cost that you have incurred over the time of your entrepreneurship.

In such instances, the first persons to quit are the ones who were already confused about their decision and backed up themselves with some exit route. It is usual to happen within the first six to 18 months of the entrepreneurial journey. In the first place, these people just get into the scene without much idea of the hardships ahead. When the picnic mood expires, they find themselves in initial difficulties and trip off pretty quickly by joining back to jobs. However, this is also appreciable that they have tried something out and could take a quick call about their liking and priorities fairly quickly.

In entrepreneurship, the more you keep the exit routes open; the more difficult it will be to sustain it. In such a case, every time you get into difficulty; rather than putting your energies into solving the problems (or at least ride the challenging period out), you tend to fight yourself on the possibility to move out of the business. The moment you become confused, your enthusiasm and positive energy will significantly decline. Your body language will announce your lack of energy to people around you, which in turn will falter their confidence in you.

So if you are in this 'confused' path with the mentality of 'if anything clicks' within a short period, or just trying out to 'do business' while you are searching for a better job, it's highly likely that you won't get anywhere with this effort, except losing your time, energy, and money!

Relevant quote:

Thom Browne (American fashion designer and entrepreneur): "When people have too many choices, they make bad choices."

66. It's not a 100-meter sprint, rather a marathon

Entrepreneurship is a tricky matter. Success comes to a few very quickly and for the rest, it takes a great test of patience. For many, the flashy stories of successful entrepreneurs and their apparent lifestyle is a factor behind taking up entrepreneurship. In recent times, the concept of entrepreneurship has been romanticized so much by the 'entrepreneurial evangelists' that quite a good lot of people are trying to become one. They are doing so being fresh out of the oven after college/graduation or leaving stable corporate jobs in search of the golden goose.

A group of entrepreneurs can raise early investment. They apparently become highly 'successful' with flashy offices, phenomenal growth, and extravagant lifestyles. This view is well enough to swing up the heads of many wannabe entrepreneurs. They start to consider it too easy to establish a startup and then sell off the company to a giant competitor for millions of dollars. One matter they don't understand is that behind those glitzy outcomes that are visible now, are lurking many months (maybe years) of hard toil and sufferings.

Before embarking on the journey of entrepreneurship, you have to have a clear understanding of what you are putting yourself into. You get a somewhat good picture after you are done with the business plan and cash flow analysis. Here you get the insight that your product will not be established just 'eventually'; rather will require a lot of effort, stress, cost, and coordination. At any point in time, your anticipated growth may be stalled because of one or two individuals; and you can't do much about it.

A person came to me with an equity offer. He asked me to develop a 'winning' product that he wants to sell off with millions of dollars (right after its being developed) and become super-rich. Apparently, he was ready to invest 'some money' in it. I candidly replied in negative and mentioned that it takes quite a lot of time, effort, and money to develop a product. It takes even more to make a mark in the market to get noticed by others and get acquired accordingly. I am not sure if he bought my words!

So, my final words in this section are, if you want to become an entrepreneur, you need to get on the track with a mentality to run a long marathon, not a quick sprint. If you are not too lucky!

Relevant quote:

Bill Gates (American business magnate, investor, author, philanthropist, humanitarian, and principal founder of Microsoft Corporation): "Success is a lousy teacher, it seduces smart people to thinking they can't lose."

67. Patience is critical

For a rare few ones, entrepreneurship can bring in quick results, in a matter of months for some. However, for the rest, it can be a long journey. It might take even a few years to settle down your business and get to bring in some money home (after paying all the expenses like salary, rent, etc.). The interesting part is, you will always feel that success is just around the corner. That motivation will drive you to face all the challenges. However, once you reach that 'corner', you will find a newer challenge that might postpone your expected cash flow further.

I started my entrepreneurial journey thinking we will break into positive cash flow within the first six months. However, even after five years of operation, I was yet to reach that point. As I mentioned, we started by establishing a software company in 2014, spent two years in different R&D and outsourcing works. However, in 2016, I put all my focus to develop a single software product and gathered my tech team around it.

In 2017, I completed the MVP (minimum viable product) and I had good hopes that my company would be able to successfully get a few customers and get into positive cash flow by the year-end. Sadly, the reality was different as the customers wanted more. The following years (2018 and 2019), it was a similar story as well. Even though facing a bit better situation in cash flow; I am still working hard to get into a positive cash flow. I am almost done developing the full phase 1 product as per client directions, and I am trying my best to get as many paying clients on board as possible. Nonetheless, no one knows what is waiting for me in the coming days!

It has been a turn off for all my partners that it's taking too long to get the business on its own feet. Reasons like timely investment shortage, diverting focus on too many things in the first two years, failure of the tech team(s) to deliver as per expectation etc. contributed to this delay. Like I said, I had to trash my software product source codes thrice before I could get hold of a tech team that delivered right, and I worked with the same team for the next 3 years.

Even though multiple partners were on board the operational management team when the startup began. Yet when the reality settled in and made it clear that success will not come quick and easy; they started to leave the management positions and decided to watch it from a safe distance. They preferred to be a member of the board of directors, but not as operationally involved management members. In the end, I was the only one, the most insanely patient and unreasonably hopeful partner of the lot, who remained there to drive the boat to success. I am sure they will continue to watch from a distance until success is reached.

This scenario is particularly true if you get yourself into developing a product. Product development takes a long time, requires a high level of investment, and takes continuous testing to ensure a product-market fit. First, you need to pour in your time and money, manage your tech team to develop an MVP, get the product to the market and sell it to earn some money. You need to ensure that you can provide the needed cash as long as it requires until your product starts earning enough to cover its own cost. Moreover, there's a mile's gap between earning your first revenue and earning your first profit (after covering all the expenses). Then it takes even more to generate sustainable profit. It's quite a regular scene where the entrepreneurs calculate the period wrong and run out of cash with no functioning product in hand.

This above scenario isn't always applicable for service-driven outsourcing based companies. They usually do not require heavy investment at the beginning and can afford to scale up once they get more orders in hand. My younger brother, who started his digital marketing agency a year earlier than me, is now running a fairly stable business since 2017. He now has more than 50 employees and earning a decent profit. Whereas, by being a product-driven company, I am still running the show with seven employees with no profit even after more than five years of operation.

Now you may ask an inevitable question, why on earth have I chosen the more difficult and much riskier path? I'll be very honest, the first reason is that I didn't know it would be so hard and take so much time, effort, and uncertainty! It took me two years to grasp the matter (where I had all the options to dump it and move away, but I continued), and since then I have been pushing the agenda for another three years.

The second reason is that a product-driven company is likely to have a more sustainable revenue than average outsourcing-based companies. From the ROI perspective, it's also more likely to earn a better rate of return by investing in a product-driven company than an outsourcing based company. If you are skeptic about my judgment, then look at all the recent big buck takeovers, the eyebrow-raising prices are all lead by product-driven companies.

Entrepreneurship might not be the field for you if you are too much of a veni-vidi-vici type of a person. There will be unforeseen hardships, showstoppers, unfair competitions, last-minute deal breaks, and many more to dampen your spirit. You have to be patient if you want to be successful!

Relevant quote:

Unknown: "Patience is not about waiting, but the ability to keep a good attitude while waiting."

68. Money is very important, but you need a bigger motivation

As I mentioned before, among all the motivation factor, financial motivation drives the entrepreneur most to cross all the hurdles on the way. On the same note, I would like to add that only financial motivation is not enough. If it was everything, you would not even consider quitting the job in the first place!

An entrepreneur is not only driven by money. As an entrepreneur, you are most likely to be driven by other factors like independence of work, be your own boss, high ambition, create something of your own, etc. Without being monetarily sound, all these factors will get weak and along the way fall short. Down the road, if you take all these factors out and keep the financial one only, it most probably will not make any sense either.

For example, even after five-plus years of entrepreneurship, I have not been able to reach the income level that I used to earn as a job holder. This is deterring me from a lot of pleasure and luxuries I used to have before quitting the job. It certainly plays as a demotivating factor for me at times. However, saying so, I am fully enjoying my entrepreneurial journey owing to the variety of value-adding work I am doing. The fact that I am trying to create my brand is also a motivating factor for me.

I previously mentioned of having a dream that will drive you through the tough times. I have a very clear dream of what I want to achieve in the next 10 and 20 years, and how I want to pass my retirement days. I know how much money I will need for a comfortable living keeping all my intended luxuries and philanthropic activities around. Interestingly, after establishing my IT startup, and consultancy services as a secondary income source, I was approached by several organizations who have proactively shown interest to take me in. They offered me with up to 2.5X the salary I used to get in my previous job. However, I decided to hold on to my dream and continue pushing forward with all the financial barriers. So, at least for me, immediate financial gain does not seem to be that big of a motivating factor. I am rather interested on sustainable good, modest, and honorable living than a short term flashy one.

Relevant quote:

Wayne Dyer (American self-help author and a motivational speaker): "Successful people make money. It's not that people who make money become successful, but that successful people attract money. They bring success to what they do."

69. The higher you were, the harder will be the adjustment

As a job quitting entrepreneur, you have many alignments to make before settling in the new role. Among the very first shocks you have to face is the absence of salary at the end of the month. The compelling challenge is even though your cash inflow stops; the outflow does not reduce much.

Throughout your job tenure, you have developed your spending habits as per your income level and much of which is of a fixed nature (e.g. house rent, kid's school fees, etc.). The higher you were in your job ladder, the more benefits you used to get translating over your lifestyle. The fact that your earning has hit a slump now as a new entrepreneur, will not necessarily mean that you will be able to cut down your expenses in similar proportion.

It is unlikely for you to shift from a certain standard of living to reduce your expenses at the drop of a hat. You may curb your habit of eating out in fine dining restaurants with your family every fortnight. There, most likely, is a very slim chance of making major decisions like changing the school of your children and moving to a cheaper neighborhood if you have an intentional career shift to become an entrepreneur. It will also create immense social and mental pressure from your friends and family.

I think quite a good portion of senior officials who emerge as entrepreneurs with a deliberate career shift, fall into a struggle to adjust to the new situation. They try out new things, spend a lot on their ideas and projects. However, when the actual cash flow turns out to be way less than anticipated or taking much more time than the anticipated period; it hits on their expensive lifestyles' bottom-line. They face a potential tuned-down lifestyle to cope with the cash shortage. This has a direct impact on their morale when faced with potential humiliation and compromised social image. Lack of resilience in this phase will mean getting back to the job again.

So, if you dream to be an entrepreneur, I recommend you to leave your job at a comparatively younger age. This shall allow you some scope to experiment with your career. You should leave your job before your salary becomes too high in the current market context. You should leave before you get accustomed to a high-end lifestyle. Quit before having posh apartments and cars, corporate membership in prestigious clubs, and expensive private schools for your children. The sooner you leave your job to become an entrepreneur, the lower will be the cost to maintain your standard of living and help you to adapt faster to the new 'reduced' lifestyle.

When I left my job, my gross salary was already hitting six-digit figures in the local currency. It was an above-average paycheck at my stage. As I left my job with some exit package, I had the luxury to sustain my lifestyle with my stored fund for a year and a half or so. By the time the stored money was completely depleted, I was able to establish myself as a corporate trainer. This pulled me through afterward. The thing that helped me a lot was my son being at a very early stage of school back then. Thus, I was able to keep the school expenses low from the very beginning. On top of that, my already comparatively lower profile lifestyle also helped me to contain my costs to a certain level.

Nonetheless, I had to forego my love for tourism for the first four years where I had to spend every penny with extreme caution. Even with funds in my account, we (me and my wife) had markedly reduced our lifestyle. Even when we ate out once in a while, we limited ourselves to comparatively lower-priced restaurants, crossing out the fine dining restaurants where we used to go before. We also stopped giving gifts to our near and dear ones on special occasions. I also stopped paying my apartment rent to my father (I live as a tenant in my father owned apartment) with the condition that I will cover them up when I again start generating enough cash! It has been the biggest unfair advantage I got as a job quitting entrepreneur, which others may not have.

During my job life, I could afford to spend a few thousand bucks in a random unplanned outing. Later as an entrepreneur I gradually had to stop most of the outings with my friend circle and reduce social interaction as they cost me money. I was cutting corners at every possible step. This created a distance with my friend circle who got used to not getting me in the gatherings and slowly accepted that

I won't be participating with them in the near future. Overall it stirred my way of life big times, yet I was able to sustain this shock as I could manage the minimum cost with the income that I got to generate from my part time involvements.

While I was fully involved in developing a software product for the local market, I have not been able to draw a salary from my IT firm. We did not have any sound investor fund and I had to take personal and institutional loans to pay my employees' salaries up till a certain stage. It was simply not feasible to take my own salary from the borrowed money. So, I decided to try and sustain myself with whatever income I can generate from my part time involvements. Luckily, I could adapt well with this minimal lifestyle as I already maintained a comparatively modest lifestyle since my job days.

Just one example will make things very clear. As mentioned earlier I got an exit package from my previous organization and it helped me immensely to find some breathing space and give me investment capacity. Besides myself, 180+ other employees of the organization quit with exit packages. Among the around 60 persons who decided to become entrepreneurs. Only four have survived after four years (including myself). The rest have quit their entrepreneurial dream and got jobs in the country or abroad.

So, the thought of entrepreneurship and being your own boss is romantic; starting a business can be exciting; yet holding on to make it successful is very difficult.

Relevant quote:

Indira Gandhi (Former Indian politician, stateswoman and a central figure of the Indian National Congress): "Life is a continuous process of adjustment."

70. You can't get a business up with a full stomach

That's purely my own philosophy. To develop a business from scratch requires super dedication and commitment. You need to be able to chase your dream with every bit of energy. That energy comes from hunger for success. Being an entrepreneur, you need to have that insatiable hunger for you and your company's success. You have to be hungry enough to beat all the difficulties, down times, and negativities that will revolve around you during your entrepreneurial journey.

A prime factor that will drive you to create and sustain that hunger is financial ambition. You need to be looking forward to quenching your financial thirst and dream about your new venture. You need to believe that your actions will eventually put you on the right track to living the lifestyle you dreamt of all along. This belief will help you overcome the impossible obstacles that you would otherwise try to bypass.

However, this motivation does not come easy. As I mentioned before, you need to be ready to sacrifice a lot of resource, comfort, and immediate enjoyment to prioritize the long-term goal. Sometimes these sacrifices may become too big and put you in a cross-road: whether to move forward or not. Your inner positive strength from that thirst to achieve your financial ambition will serve as your driving force at this time.

Quite a lot of people start their own business with much enthusiasm, but fail to make it successful by giving up abruptly. A good number of people start their own business while having their regular job. After the initial struggle, a time comes when the business demands more time and dedication from its owner(s). That point is very tricky. As an entrepreneur with a job on the side, you won't feel like getting out of your comfort zone to quit it for the money it pays. Whereas your venture demands your time with not much immediate returns in sight. You need to take a leap of faith by having confidence in the business. You must reckon the risk of it to click and eventually generate much more (or at least similar) cash compared to your existing job.

THE IDEAL QUITTER

This is where the wannabe entrepreneurs falter most of the time and decide to play it safe by focusing on financial security. I have observed many such cases and thus don't find interest to hear any business ideas from fully involved job holders. They plan to run their business side by side and plan to hop once it starts to generate 'enough cash'. The catch is, the business is highly unlikely to grow and return profits while you are on the job. Your existing company (where you are working right now) is not paying salary for your most productive hours of the day for nothing. Unless you or one of your partners quit his or her job and start to contribute the most productive time to the business, it wouldn't flourish.

Relevant quote:

Unknown: "If it is important to you, you will find a way. If not, you will find an excuse."

71. Commit time in additional businesses with caution:

While starting a new business, just like you searched for suitable partners, other entrepreneurs are searching for one too. We all know that getting a good partner with the right integrity and mental alignment is a very critical matter that might become the success or failure factor of the business. As a result, after a certain time, if you can establish your positive image and intention; you will regularly receive partnership offers from different people.

While in one part, the fact that people are approaching you with partnership offers is mentally fulfilling. It is an indication that you have established a certain level of goodwill in the market. On the other part, it also presents opportunities to create further assets in addition to your already existing startup. Properly choosing the right partnership might open the door for even more riches than your original startup idea.

In this phase, you must assess the partnership offer seriously. You have to think diligently on whether this offer matches with your overall strategic goal, personality, and capability. You also have to examine if these are aligned with the vision, mentality, and integrity of the other party. Cross-check what is expected of you upon becoming a partner. If your interest as well as the bandwidth to contribute in that business matches, next you should assess whether the other party intends to utilize your capabilities for long term or short term.

If your input is required for a very short term; I would suggest not to accept any equity offer*ing*. Rather offer short term consultancy to give them direction and walk away with immediate benefits like cash, if they can afford to. You may differ with my opinion. I believe staying in a company without much long-term contribution will in due time create an uncomfortable equation. In such a case, the other contributing members will be questioning your share of the equity. After all, it is human nature to remember and put more emphasis on recent history and forgetting the previous ones.

Moreover, you know your startup better than anyone else. You should be able to gauge whether you have any additional bandwidth at all to contribute to other businesses. If yes, in which format? Can you get involved in operational activities? Do you have that excess capacity to hold a particular position there? If not, then should you contribute from a strategic position and play an advisory role only? Will that be accepted by the other party? How will your existing partners react to this decision? There are many factors to consider before you commit your time to other business. If that is a major call, it's always better to discuss with your existing partners.

Getting into more ventures will come with the potential to improve your future assets. However, saying so, additional activities might do more harm than good. You have to assess whether your own created 'baby' venture is in a good enough condition (or at least on the right track) to allow you to divert your attention to other businesses. If it's still not in the right shape, and you get your hands off from the steering wheel, it might cause a potential disaster, inflicting a decisive damage to your business. It will draw your startup backward and disqualify quite a good level of achievements that you have done so far. Failure to prioritize properly will hamper your business and future planning by large.

You have a very limited timeframe to get involved in business activities. Think hard before you agree to commit your time and money in other ventures. You may already be involved in other short-term cash-earning activities to meet your monthly expenses. You may have invested a lot of time and other resources in projects. You should commit to something else only when you are confident that it will add value to your long- or short-term goal. You need to be sure that this involvement will not damage your current business. In alignment, you should ensure bringing in and setting up people who are competent, confident, honest, and motivated enough to execute operations without your direct supervision.

I follow the same principle while judging a new business involvement proposal. I always focus on whether it is aligned with my vision and if I share a comfort zone with the potential partner. This comfort comes from the other person's integrity, vision, team player mentality and many other attributes. I have let quite a few potential high yielding opportunities slip just because I felt I cannot deliver the expected time. I am the full-time CEO of a tech startup and also engaged in separate short-term projects and activities. Committing to run yet another company is just not feasible as it will take a toll on me and my own company's future. In my current circumstance, I only consider to engage myself as a partner where I can play a strategic role. I can direct, and advice where there are other people to run the show!

Relevant quote:

Peter F. Drucker (Austrian-born American management consultant, educator, and author, whose writings contributed to the philosophical and practical foundations of the modern business corporation): "Unless a commitment is made, there are only promises and hopes; but no plans."

72. Family is everything; deprive them within limit

A few of the reasons that are most likely to turn you into an entrepreneur are to be your own boss, freedom of work, not bound by any routine activities and maybe a few more. No matter what the reason is; once you get fully involved in your new set business, it turns out to be a very interesting game. Your full attention will be diverted to nurture your 'infant baby' to sustainability.

Very soon you will find this 'baby' to be the center of all your attention (just like a mother feels for her child). Just like a mother, you will feel the pulse of the business, panic with the slightest sign of any difficulty, and the small steps of successes will bring immense joy. When you see the business grow slowly, you will be obsessed with it, sometimes even love it out of proportion and without any logic. You just cannot compare the sense of achievement of watching your baby business slowly turning into a profitable one with anything else.

In this period, it's very easy to lose focus from yourself and your family's wellbeing. Very often, you will find yourself working 10 to 14 hours a day and with hardly any weekend to take rest. Every day is a working day! Out of over-enthusiasm, you tend to deprive yourself of much-needed rest (when your body recovers from stress-related internal injuries). You also deprive yourself of the company of your immediate family members like your spouse and kids, parents, and close relatives. I have even come across an apparent entrepreneur who was boasting of not attending any family event for the three years since he started his own business!

It's rather normal that you will get consumed with your self-imposed works and have very little scope of work-life balance. Nonetheless, you should try to minimize the impact as soon as possible. It's okay to work like hell for the first few years, and you have to set your expectations accordingly. However, once you start to settle down a bit and assign roles to people to do regular work, you should have some spare time in your hands. You should have some time to spend with your family as well; at least better than the initial phase of your entrepreneurship. However, don't get confused with one of my previous sections where I mentioned that you need to be proactive and search out works to ensure the sustainability of your business. This point does not contradict, rather compliments the thought of giving more time to your family. Having stability at home will impact your sustainability in your business in some way or another. Moreover, being proactive at work means more readiness and less firefighting on emergency issues, which ultimately means more stability and work-life balance.

In my case, I live in Dhaka city, the capital of Bangladesh that is (in-) famous for the traffic jam. I had to spend a few hours on the road daily while commuting from home to office. Riding my bicycle was faster than traveling on public transport (or any three and above wheeler to be more precise) for a 17 km ride! Added with my initial entrepreneurial work load; I had to leave home at around 8 to 8.30 am and took up till 11 pm to reach back home after work. It was highly stressful for me and I could feel the stress of my parents seeing me in this situation. It also impacted my wife and little son (he was around 4 when I started my own business) as I got back home only to sleep. Our face to face interaction was limited to a maximum of an hour a day. Only the entrepreneurial spirit held me together and kept me out of burnout.

However, after crossing the 5 years mark in entrepreneurship, I have settled down a bit. Even with all my financial challenges, I can feel that my business has found its path. Although it is still not close to becoming a successful venture, yet it is heading in a certain direction. With employees set in places, I feel that I can now relax a bit and spend some time for myself. On top of that, I could afford to bring my office very close to home, reducing my daily commute in the traffic jam. All this effort combined; I have managed time to start writing this book (which was only a dream in the first few years) to share my learning with everyone. My son and I sometimes go out for around an hour-long evening walk in the local park. We have even managed to have a family vacation that we could not afford in the first four years!

My utmost request to you is to identify your ultimate priorities in life. No matter how much you are engaged with your business; in the end, it might fall apart. Over years of hard toil and dealing with high stress, it's crucial that you do not get burned out. This is also one of the major causes why entrepreneurs fail. Down the line, the things that will remain constant with you are the most important factors of your life. Your personal wellbeing and your family are the permanent factors that will stick with you forever. Whether you like it or not, you have to remain loyal to them; and take good care of them as well.

There should not come a day when you look back and repent on why you have not given more time to your parents, spouse, children, and other family members.

Relevant quote:

Jon Acuff (American author of five books): "Dear entrepreneurs, you can start a thousand businesses, launch 100 projects, and take dozens of companies public, but you only have one shot at being part of your kid's childhood. Your kid doesn't care about your platform, they care about your presence."

73. Be Positive and don't look back

By now, you should have properly grasped that entrepreneurship is not as romantic as it sounds and has its due share of both sides of the coin: pain and excitement. However, if you want to be a successful entrepreneur, you have to be able to manage the disappointments and stay focused on your goals. At times, you cannot but feel down with a sudden downturn of events; but you cannot afford to be demoralized for a long time.

As a job quitting entrepreneur, your journey will most significantly get affected by a dampened spirit. Nothing hurts the spirit like looking back and asking yourself "how better I was in the good old days, and where I am right now". You will always have the option to look back to how good things were in the past, what sort of position and power you had, and what sort of stability you have sacrificed to start your own business. You are the person who is to 'blame' for this situation. The worst outcome of this activity is a destroyed morale from within which no one can help to rebuild.

Remember, you chose this path, and looking back is only harming the future. If you decide to cut short your entrepreneurial journey and get back to a secured job, there's no harm in it. Delaying will only increase your sufferings. I would suggest you to not get into the state of 'escalation of commitment'. It roughly means to continue doing what you were doing even though internally you feel that you made a mistake. Do not linger in the journey just because others will laugh at you. An entrepreneur will not be able to move much with a shattered energy level. Just do not waste time by remaining in between.

At this point, you might ask me, "How do I keep my spirits up even when things are not going in my way?" My answer would be to look at the big picture and see where you are right now on the path to success. Entrepreneurs hold a 'relentlessly hopeful' spirit! This helps to cope with stressful situations and remain positive in tough times. You have to do the math of your winning probability on this road. If you even have a fair share of it in your mind, you should continue.

THE IDEAL QUITTER

You have to hold on to the dream of success and the perks of becoming a successful entrepreneur in your mind. Think of what you want to achieve and how would you like to enjoy your life when things will be easier. Think of your plans that you want to carry on when you succeed. These happy thoughts will give you a much-needed respite from the negative energy that will consume you if you remain unchecked.

Relevant quote:

Hillary Clinton (American politician, diplomat, lawyer, writer, and public speaker): "Every moment wasted looking back, keeps us from moving forward."

74. Don't let the negativity of other people dampen your energy

Entrepreneurship is a tough choice and there is every possibility that you might fail. Irrespective of how talented you are and how much positive energy you have, you still can be unlucky enough to fail in your venture. You might develop a product too ahead of the market, or your partner(s) might just not cooperate with you enough at a critical time. You may be unfortunate enough to not to get an investor for a seemingly great MVP just because you live in a not so affluent economy. Although it might be a completely different scenario if you live in a developed economy where venture capitalists are much more hopeful and positive risk-takers.

As if the possibility itself is not enough, there will be people around you who will have a close eye to see what happens next. If you win, they will remain quiet; however, with every downturn and failure, they will come and tease you. They will happily say, "see! I knew you would fail!" These people are either directly or indirectly talking against you, your capabilities, your efforts, your venture, and your dreams.

No matter how much you hate to have such people around you, you are bound to face these in the society. Some people will be talking about you and how big a mistake you have made by not re-entering into a stable job or (even a bigger mistake by) quitting that steadfast corporate job in the first place.

The best thing to do in such a case is to know who they are and keep away from them as much as possible. If they are your close family members, don't share any information with them, unless it's a good and inspiring one! Every negative story or small failure will give them more fuel to demotivate you with their words and deplete your positive energy level.

I will strongly suggest you to surround yourself with similar minded people during this time; preferably entrepreneurs of the same bracket. Try to find one or two well-wishing senior entrepreneurs as your mentors with whom you can share your thoughts, ideas, challenges. Develop your entrepreneur friend circle as only an entrepreneur will understand the pain of another one and suggest realistic solutions. It will help you to de-stress during downtimes and will help you to know others' viewpoints on how to navigate through them. An enlightened and positive friend circle will work wonders in rejuvenating a rather shaken spirit. This circle will also help each other to solve their problems.

Relevant quote:

Unknown: "Negative people need drama like oxygen. Stay positive, it will take their breath away."

75. Luck is a major factor

To build a successful business, there is no alternative to hard work and determination. You can hardly find any entrepreneur who just got lucky and got rich. Even if so, the entrepreneur has to get his or her due credit to come up with the solution to a problem well in time to be able to be at the right place at the right time. Saying so, if you are a true entrepreneur you have to acknowledge the 'luck' factor. For apparently no (or very remote) reason whether you get lucky or super unlucky, might either make or break your business.

Let's take the example of Paytm, a mobile financial service (MFS) application, based in India. Paytm started off as a mere mobile recharge website in 2010. The company was already a fairly large player in the market in 2016. Luckily, the company hit a jackpot with a government decision taken overnight. To flush out black money from the market, the Indian Government banned 500- and 1000-Rupee notes that created a major cash crisis in the market. [6]

Without having sufficient cash in their pocket, people had to turn their faces to MFS for paying their dues. It worked as a direct blessing for the relevant players in the market, especially Paytm. Within one year (Oct'16 to Nov'17), their user base doubled from 140 million to 270 million. The company's valuation also doubled to USD 7 billion since their last round of investment, where they raised a massive investment of USD 1.4 billion in May 2017.

On the other hand, you may have the best product in the world. If a sudden political and economic downturn looms over, it may disrupt your business to extinction. In my case, one of my startups, Humac Lab, developed a seemingly ground breaking mobile application called 'Madviser' in 2015. Madviser helped the users to reduce their mobile and internet bills based on their calling and mobile internet browsing pattern. The machine learning operation was so good that in extreme cases some users were able to save up to 80% of their mobile bills. In the backend, this was a major data generator from where the mobile telecom operators and relevant research firms could get huge benefit with real time usage-based information of the cumulative subscribers.

As the investment eco-system was (and still is) not much developed in Bangladesh, we could not raise any investment. As a result, we had to move toward self-sustainability ASAP. On our quest, we approached 'Airtel', an Indian mobile telecom operating in Bangladesh who was the 4th ranking player (among 5 competitors) in the contemporary market.

As we were helping the users to find the cheapest solution, and Airtel was the cheapest operator in the market. When we started moving toward the commercial discussion with Airtel and agreed on a pilot, we were confident that the future was bright. However, in an unfortunate turn of events for us, right then Airtel centrally merged with the 3rd ranking mobile operator Robi to become the 2nd largest operator combined. Once the decision was made, naturally, all the new developments and initiatives got halted on the spot for an unlimited time. Our hope to become self-sustainable with Madviser came to an abrupt end. We had no other way but to shelf this product and discontinue investing in it. Luck played a hard turn on us!

Nonetheless, I believe the harder and smarter you work, the better fits the luck on your side.

Relevant quote:

Barbara Sher (speaker, career/lifestyle coach, and author): "The amount of good luck coming your way depends on your willingness to act."

76. Be passionate

The initial entrepreneurial drive does not take much time to disappear as the reality sets in. In this period, it takes more than regular enthusiasm and logic to continue moving forward. Sometimes, you may feel completely hopeless with the uncertainty as everything seems to be working against you!

If money is the only motivator behind your entrepreneurial spirit, I must say that your enthusiasm will not take much time to disappear. Even if you manage an early investment and get your investors agree to pay you a fat salary, it will fall flat if you are not successful in generating sustainable profit. So, personal income (I am not saying 'asset') generation should not become the focal point of an entrepreneur, at least in the short run.

In this period, you will probably see your friends and previous colleagues leading a better life in terms of cash. You would feel you're missing out on all the fun by choosing to build a 'business' that might be taking much more time to become profitable than anticipated. Gradually you will find yourself avoiding the friends' gathering just as you can't afford the additional cost and slowly start to fade out from their lives. Your friends will also know it and slowly start ignoring you in meetups. Soon enough you will get notified about the friends' past gatherings from social media after the fun pics are posted! This is a tough matter to digest, to say the least!

Your family members will also turn out to be a bit more curious about you as they are not sure where you are heading. You might face uncomfortable questions about the direction of your business. Your parents and other well-wishers might come up with pieces of advice on alternatives for you as they think you might get into depression if you push further into the never-ending battle. You might find yourself avoiding even general discussions with your family members. You will find yourself deserted and fighting an uphill climb on your own. If you want to cry, you will face with comments like, "See, I told you before", "I knew you couldn't", "get a job" etc. that are sure to not give you much comfort!

However, nothing else will matter if you are truly focused on your business and making it successful. 'Passion' is defined as something you so much enjoy doing that you would do it anyway even if you were not paid for it. So, firstly you need to rule out immediate financial motivation and jot down the motivating factors that will drive you through the difficult times. You need to envision your future and believe in what you are doing and trying to establish.

For me, I dream of creating a product that will rule the world in its category. I dream of employing around 250 people (Currently I have only 8!) in my company within the next five years. I dream of having a positive impact on my customers' lives so much that they will proactively come up with their problems and ask us to design the solutions. You might ask, "So, money is not anywhere in your motivation checklist?" I will strongly disagree with that. I believe money will automatically follow if my business is successful. A company cannot sustain with a world-leading product and employ a good number of people without making a sustainable profit.

Relevant quote:

John C. Maxwell (American author, speaker, and pastor who has written many books, primarily focusing on leadership): "A great leader's courage to fulfill his vision comes from passion, not position."

77. Push to the end, but know when to quit

For some, entrepreneurship is a game of struggle, endurance, and attrition. If you are not committed to seeing it till the end, it's likely to fall apart with no profit. You need to commit to giving your best effort and make sure that no stones were left unturned, and quit only then. It's best to accept defeat and move on when things are not moving in your favor even after trying all the options. Try to ensure that there are no gaps in your effort before you quit, or else you will start questioning your commitment as an entrepreneur.

It's not necessary to push every endeavor until the end. If you feel your resolution to stick with a product or startup is shook up, not showing proper prospect anymore, or simply the passion is not there anymore, then you should close down the venture. It will be the best course of action to quit rather than continue half-heartedly.

Relevant quote:

Unknown: "Don't quit because something went wrong. Quit because you tried your hardest and nothing made it better."

78. Keep praying to the Almighty

Entrepreneurship is a mode of work where you must deal with uncertainty every day; a lot of which are out of your control. Bearing too much pressure may lead to hypertension and other physical and mental ailments. If you get caught up in finger-pointing by finding faults in every failure (either from your side or others.) You will get too worked up. Others will eventually reciprocate (be it justified or not) the blaming. It will shatter the work environment and the relationship between key stakeholders. You should have a proper monitoring system to ensure the due diligence of your deliverables. It's taken that trying to do the right things and getting the right things done are not the same. Despite trying your best, anything can go wrong. Then you have to admit that things were beyond your control. It was not meant to be, it's as simple as that.

You must be as much diligent as possible. After doing your part, if you believe in God, then keep praying to him so that everything goes as smooth as possible. In case of a mishap, the sooner you accept that God knows best, and you are given this hard time for a reason (and understanding that reason is beyond the comprehension of human capabilities); the sooner you will be at peace! It will enable you to focus on your next deliverables.

Although I try to be a practicing Muslim from a young age, I have personally felt a deeper connection with my almighty, Allah, since I became an entrepreneur. Over the first five years of my endeavor, I have deeply felt that my actions are being observed by him. He directly intervened whenever I became tired of fighting against the odds. These last-minute helps are truly remarkable and sometimes even make me feel happy-go-lucky. Getting access to a government grant (that was approved months back but was being delayed due to red tapes) right when I was not finding any way to pay the salaries was a blessing. It was miraculous when one of my clients called me up to pay a long-pending due (that even I forgot) just when I was struggling to meet day to day expenses including the payment of my son's school fees. Such incidents have become so regular, that nowadays, I do not even get worried about costs! I know that Allah will find a way. I need to keep trying and keep faith in the mercy of the Almighty!

On the face of failure, deep down I feel that an apparent disappointment might have saved me from a bigger misery in the future. It may have provided me with critical learning that will make me a better person with better decision-making skills. Instead of panicking, I always know that something better is waiting for me in the coming days. With such appeasing thoughts, you just cannot afford to become an intolerant, impatient, distressed, and negative person! Nonetheless, you need to continue doing positive work with all your abilities as well. Sitting idle and expecting a timely shower of good luck and blessings will not help I believe!

Relevant quote:

Unknown: "Wake up. Pray. Hustle."

Conclusion

Entrepreneurship is the name of a very romantic yet very adventurous, challenging, and risky journey. Quite a good number of people have reached their full potential through this path, yet 100 times more people might have lost a good deal while embarking on this journey and have been forgotten. You need to take very calculative risks and deeply assess your capabilities and analyze your SWOT before taking on any such challenge.

I have seen people with mediocre standing in their jobs, yet being reluctant to become entrepreneurs as they do not feel prepared for such a challenge. I respect and appreciate their point of view of not going with the trend by understanding own strengths an weaknesses; thus curtailing unnecessary pressure.

I have tried to share my approx. USD 500,000 worth lessons taken over the first five years of entrepreneurship. I hope that with this knowledge you can start your business and walk down this path in a much more effective and efficient manner than I could. However, even if you follow all the above steps, there is every possibility that you might fail in your current venture. Nonetheless, this is all about entrepreneurship and positive attitude where you have to rise from the ashes and start moving again. You should keep your priorities intact and work with honesty and smart efforts to exceed the opportunity cost of leaving the job behind. You have to start a new life that will lead to fulfillment in your life in the context of a better standard of living and/ or a better peace of mind.

Entrepreneurship is a life full of determination and dream; where it is said, **"Entrepreneurs live a few years of their lives like most people won't so that they can spend the rest of their lives like most people can't!"**

Bonus part

Ten signs that you will be an early quitting entrepreneur

In recent times, a good number of people are taking entrepreneurship as their preferred career path. Great future waits for those who will succeed in this journey, without any doubt. With a bright dream of 'doing something of my own' and 'building my own empire', these people embark on this route. They choose a line of work, communicate with their near and dear ones within their network, and start asking for works/ projects. Some people put trust in the newcomers and their abilities and assign work to them. This is the standard way of an entrepreneurial start.

Plenty of entrepreneurs fail to become successful due to different reasons. However, they do so upon giving their best efforts being aware of the high-risk scenario. Nonetheless, as unfortunate as it may sound, many drop off at an early stage. At the initial level of entrepreneurial stress, they quit their endeavor. In the process, quite often, they jeopardize the project(s) in hand and create much trouble and headache for the ones who entrusted them with their important tasks.

No matter how much justification there may be, these untimely quits do a lot of harm to the relationships (because the early works come through relationships) with their customers, create good dents in future credibility and trustworthiness of the entrepreneur. It may make the path of future entrepreneurs more difficult when people get wired to doubt new entrepreneurs for some who quit mid-track.

Being a full-time entrepreneur since 2014, I also have tried to help other new entrepreneurs by making them my value chain partners and service providers. To my dismay I have come across a few such failed entrepreneurs who have slipped in their part and have contributed to a significant loss in my business.

For instance, an ex-colleague of mine (from a mobile telecom company) approached us after quitting his job and offered his services. We assigned him a task as an outsourced service provider trusting in his capabilities for a two-month project. One fine morning, we heard that he has joined another job. Initially, he showed positive energy that no matter what, he will deliver our project. When this two-month project rolled out to its sixth month and we were yet to complete even 50% of it, we had to scrap it. This delay caused extensive monetary and opportunity loss for my company. I also vowed not to become the 'supporting hand' for any newer startups without properly assessing their commitment!

This and a few more incidents made me think why some entrepreneurial journeys are so short-lived. Certainly, no one wants to fail, yet few decide to take a detour and get back to their previous path very easily. After much brainstorming, I can conclude on the following traits of early quitting entrepreneurs. Knowing these traits should help others to measure their possibility of succeeding in this path before actually embarking on it with uncertainty and risk.

1. **You put a lot of weight on 'stability'**: entrepreneurship is all about high risk – high gain scenario. There may be cases where entrepreneurs get lucky to get and a handful of return in no time, yet many toil away for a longer time to reach that point. Think ten times before choosing to be an entrepreneur if you are do not have the appetite to embark on such journey or cannot take such risks, and rock your stable boat that is maintained by your salary; think ten times before you choose to try to be entrepreneur.

2. **You place personal interest and well-being way above your commitment to others**: everyone understands their interest, and there is no harm in it. However, to reach success you need to be the type of person who performs their commitment at any cost, even if it means incurring loss (up to a certain extent). If you are good at justifying your 'failure to deliver' by your standard, it's better to not take the entrepreneurship path.

3. **'Patience' is not the virtue you have**: Entrepreneurs must be patient with countless unforeseen hurdles and risks. If you are the kind of person who panics quite easily and tries to conclude an alternative path fast; then entrepreneurship is not for you. It certainly will result in many sleepless nights and high BP!

4. **You sway between your decisions**: Many people juggle between decisions and take forever to approach one. If you are one such person, then it's a bad idea to become an entrepreneur as this path will ask for a quick, firm, and sometimes instinctive decision that might fail! Why go for such tension?

5. **You always keep exit options open**: When you decide to become an entrepreneur, you should become one with a full heart and commit yourself for at least a minimum reasonable period. However, if the thought of getting back to a job is always on, then it is highly likely that you will snap at the first exposure to major difficulty and actively start searching for a job and switching to one. So, why risk losing your time and reputation then?

6. **Failure is not an option for you**: Entrepreneurship is all about learning from previous failures, getting up from disasters, and starting the journey again. If you are in such a position where you cannot accept a failure (e.g. you have a family to feed with no backup income source than your job's salary), think many times before you decide to start your romantic entrepreneurial journey.

7. **Entrepreneurial success is a 'good to have' for you**: Many of us (including me) failed at their first attempt to achieve success as an entrepreneur just because the success in it was a 'good to have' one. We depended on other sources for 'real success' (e.g. the current job). The entrepreneurship always falls behind when the time comes for some real prioritization, resulting in an early quit from the endeavor.

8. **You are not Desperate enough**: For most of the people, success does not come easily. You need to desperately search for it. If you are casual about it and (most probably) have other means of living your life, it only chalks up to not being desperate enough. So, again when the time comes, you will choose that 'other way' (most probably your existing job, or the job offer you have in your hand) over your entrepreneurial venture to thrive.

9. **Your stomach is full**: I believe in one notion, and that is 'you cannot be a successful entrepreneur with a full stomach'. You need to be hungry, really hungry! If you are not in dire need of success (be it financial, social, spiritual or in any other form), it is highly unlikely for you to pass the bumpy tests to withstand the long term toil, if required. You need that insatiable appetite for success in your venture. It will drive you to move ahead breaking all brick walls and see it through, till the end.

10. **You do not have a clear dream**: The fruits of successful entrepreneurship are great; yet usually they do not come easy and require years of dedication, hard work, and sacrifice. It is not possible to cross these hurdles if you do not have a dream large and clear enough to make these toils look like peanuts!

There are a handful of scientific researches to dissect a successful entrepreneurs' mind. I believe, of the specific traits of early quitting entrepreneurs can also be a matter of speculation and research. A reasonable person will think of both positives and negatives that may arise before actually taking this path.

I earnestly hope to see no more early quitting entrepreneurs in future!

Reference

[1] Dabbawala, *Wikipedia*, Retrieved from: https://en.wikipedia.org/wiki/Dabbawala, Date of access: 01 November 2019

[2] "Ride-Sharing in Bangladesh: Disrupting the way we commute" *IDLC Monthly Business Review,* June 2018, Retrieved from: https://idlc.com/mbr/article.php?id=125, Date of Access: 01 October 2019

[3] "Returning Customers Spend 67% More Than New Customers-You're your Customers Coming Back with a Recurring Revenue Sales Model", May 2013, Retrieved from: https://www.business.com/articles/returning-customers-spend-67-more-than-new-customers-keep-your-customers-coming-back-with-a-recurring-revenue-sales-model/). Date of Access: 01 June 2019

[4] Boskirk S.V.(March 2011),"Consumer "Ad-itudes" Stay Strong," Retrieved from: https://www.forrester.com/report/Consumer+Aditudes+Stay+Strong/-/E-RES58875#, Date of Access: 01 August 2019

[5] Franklin M.J.(May 2018),"7 social media apps you forgot about — and what happened to them," Retrieved from: https://mashable.com/2018/05/24/best-apps-you-forgot-about/, Date of access: 15 July 2019

[6] Singh K.,Mandal S.,Mahanti A.(September 2017), "OPPORTUNITY ANALYSIS: THE STORY OF PAYTM DURING DEMONETISATION," Retrieved from: https://www.researchgate.net/publication/331036463, Date of access: 20 May 2019

[7] Sutevski Dragan (November 2012), "HOW YOU CAN MEASURE BUSINESS POTENTIAL ENERGY OF YOUR BUSINESS IDEAS", retrieved from https://www.entrepreneurshipinabox.com/389/measure-business-potential-energy-ideas/, date of access: 12 April 2020

THE IDEAL QUITTER

ABOUT THE AUTHOR

Mr. Md. Mubir Mahmud Chowdhury, born in 1979, is an expert in Customer Experience Management and Direct Sales with over 16 years of professional experience. He decided to chase his entrepreneurial dream and left his corporate career in 2013 and dedicated his full time in developing multiple businesses since.

Over the years, Mr. Chowdhury's created start-ups have earned prestigious awards like Seedstars World (Bangladesh chapter), BRAC Manthan, and mBillionth South Asia etc. His start-up was also nominated among Bangladesh's top 10 IT initiatives by the government. He also works as mentor for new start-ups in different government and private initiatives.

Mr. Chowdhury is also a customer centricity professional and runs the only customer experience management consultancy firm in Bangladesh. He works as a soft skills trainer for government projects as well and has worked as a system analysis consultant for government services automation with the Prime Minister's office of the People's republic of Bangladesh.

www.ingramcontent.com/pod-product-compliance
Lightning Source LLC
Chambersburg PA
CBHW030628220526
45463CB00004B/1450